ISBN: 978-1-947863-25-5 (Paperback edition)
ISBN: 978-1-947863-26-2 (Kindle edition)
ISBN: 978-1-947863-27-9 (Audio edition)

Cover art and design by bookcoverart.com

Printed and bound in the United States of America.
First printing January 2025.

Published by Kirby Publishing, LLC
Lacey, WA 98503

SMALL BUSINESS SCHOOL

Begin Your Business Journey

By

Troy Kirby

THE
SEEDLING

"I wanted a perfect ending. Now I've learned, the hard way, that some poems don't rhyme, and some stories don't have a clear beginning, middle, and end. Life is about not knowing, having to change, taking the moment and making the best of it, without knowing what's going to happen next. Delicious Ambiguity." - Gilda Radner

THE IDEA SEED

Welcome to the idea seed of entrepreneurship. This is the beginning. The beginning of a lot of things, beyond this book. It is the beginning of your journey with me into the world of small business. I have had a lot of beginnings, middles and ends. That's simply by interacting, and observing. This is not unique to me, except that I am the one writing this book, therefore, I have the ultimate goal of relaying this information onto you, the reader. Unless this is an audio book, in which you are the listener, not the reader. See, even after the finality of something, you do have to recognize one thing: Change.

I get it. This business book is uncommon because it refuses to be absolutely dry. It forces the reader to go through various personal stories that I tell in a folksy sort of way. But the truth of the matter is simple: We learn by relatable example. The larger the corporation, the harder it is to truly relate to their struggle. But when the struggle is real, and somewhat micro, it hits home for us. It makes me lean in when I hear of a local struggle because it might be comparable to what I am going through.

One of my businesses in 2019 was not supposed to be busy. I was simply picking up a candy machine because I was sick of a vendor not filling his. I ran a family fun center at the time, Charlie's Safari, and the candy vendor would not drive throughout his territory down 120 miles every weekend to fill his candy machine. As a family fun center, we ran through a lot of things, especially loose quarters that ventured into his candy machine. And yet, he was unwilling or unable to accommodate our request that he fill it. We earned a cool 17% from his machine being on site. It was small change compared to making the kids happy that they could access hard candies that fit in the size of their tiny palms for only a quarter. Even in 2019, inflation had rendered most things more expensive than a quarter. And yet, this candy machine offered that to our family fun center attendees.

I searched on Facebook marketplace and found a U-Turn Terminator, eight candy dispenser machine available. It stood four feet tall, one foot wide, and was on a swivel. I drove the family fun center truck and trailer up to retrieve it on a Wednesday morning after my rotary meeting, excited to pay the $75 freight simply to fill the machine. Honestly, I didn't care about making money off of the machine, figured the candy was a loss leader, but if it made the kids happy, then the parents were happy, and everyone would spend more. And complain less.

The Facebook candy machine seller was 50 miles from the family fun center. I arrived there, parked out front, and listened to two people arguing inside. I wondered if I had the wrong place, but my instant message said otherwise. The man said that he would be right out. I waited. Then the twin garage doors opened. Inside the garage were four U-Turn Terminators, a ton of candy, parts and other things set in a load of boxes. The man stood six feet-two, lit up a cigarette, then eyed me for a moment.

"Sell you the whole thing for $300."

"The whole thing?"

"Yeah. Including the big red machine for candy and fake tattoos in the box over there."

It was right during this exchange that I heard a woman yelling from inside the house. She was angry, annoyed that the man standing next to me had not met some expectation. Something about the garbage or the dishes or something. That was when the man leaned in, blowing away his cigarette smoke, smiling.

"I'm selling everything. Moving to Boise tomorrow. She doesn't know it yet."

And that was how I got into the vending machine business. Throughout 2019, I generated over $1,700 on the candy that he provided me alone at the family fun center. When the 2020 COVID-19 shutdowns hit and the family fun center was forced to close forever, I put the candy machines in storage. The only one that stayed intact was Big Red, which sold candy and tattoos at the local laundromat. I gave back 17% of the gross to the owner, and it generated $3,085.75 in the time period from Oct 12, 2019 to December 2, 2023. That's $2,591.14 in net profits. I have an excel spreadsheet that details everything.

Sometimes, we do not see the beginning of something. I could have easily passed on the guy's offer to purchase the entire lot for $300. I could have removed myself from the opportunity of gaining almost $3,000 in sales from one machine alone. Because it is difficult to see the beginning of something, it's hard to witness how things generate, compound and become worth more over time. It's been a nice passive income based on one man's desire to run off like a thief in the night, escaping a situation of domestic anger for Boise or wherever the hell he ended up. All I know is that I got an unexpected business out of the deal, for less than 10% of the initial buy-in.

UNITS OF TIME

You should attempt to understand units of time. Segment out that each hour has four units. These are 15-minute periods. You can even segment out further, saying that there are 20 units of five-minute periods, within an hour. Ask yourself how much money you can gain per unit, given a specific task. Creative types will often look at generating fiction or other types of writing through five-minute periods. Just do eight periods of five minutes throughout the day. That is 40 minutes total, separated out in five minutes each hour. This assumes that you are working an eight-hour day and can take five minutes, each hour, in order to generate fiction. Now, let's extend that to how much you can make, in specialized periods, doing different tasks throughout the day.

As a person that owns a candy machine at a laundromat, I can remove all of the coins, fix any issues and refill the machine within 60 minutes. For that 40 minute period, I average about $250 by servicing that machine every three months. But notice that window of time of only 60 minutes, is now only 20 minutes per month, equaling $83.30 gross, per month. That is not a lot to exist on if that is all you are going to end up doing. But within an overall scope, that $250 gross becomes the easiest hour of pay that I may ever have. You have to think of the amount of multiples of gross income, spread out in different tasks, that can equal out into the overall income that you want.

SMALL BUSINESS SCHOOL

Let's say that I had 40 candy machines, each producing $250 every three months, and it took 60 minutes to perform the same coin removal, fix any issues and refill. That would mean 40 hours per three months, $10,000 gross total divided by 3, equaling $3,333.33 gross per month. That sounds better, but that also looks at everything achieving a perfect ratio. Assuming that there are no breakage issues with the candy machines (i.e. the human factor) or cheating (i.e. people putting in small coins such as pennies instead of quarters). Everything comes down to the understanding that nothing is perfect. You may show up one morning, only to find the entire machine is missing and someone walked off with it. Literally, picked up the machine, carried it on their shoulder, and exited out the front door. Depends on the location, which also likely wants a cut of your candy sales.

As you are factoring all of this together, this is why it is important to make supplement revenue stream assumptions. This helps build up your revenue streams into a multiple, without it being your sole source of income. Your ability to have different revenue streams, including candy machine sales, is what will help protect you. As when one revenue stream fails, the other revenue streams will help carry the weight. Much like a mechanic is also a tire dealer, also a brakes dealer, and happens to carry various versions of different car stereos or speakers. All of these are ancillaries, but they still require the mechanic to have the same type of customer: someone requiring their vehicle to be serviced. But imagine that the mechanic owns the building and has three other tenants in that building. Now, the mechanic is gaining rent from three different businesses, likely not competitors. Assume that the mechanic also places a soda pop vending machine, and other vending machines, in each of the tenant's suites. Now, the mechanic is gaining additional revenue, servicing those machines in only select periods, while also collecting rent checks which cover the building's mortgage and bottom line.

Notice how the revenue streams changed. It would likely be written into each tenant's lease. The service might be done by the mechanic or one of their employees, and it isn't more than a few standard hours of service per month or quarter. Too often, these are the opportunities that the "yes, but..." guy on your shoulder denies are available, yet there they are. A mechanic that owns a building is not merely a mechanic, but an entrepreneur with various business extensions waiting to be exploited. And it becomes the responsibility of each tenant, coupled with their own foot traffic to their own individual businesses, which feeds the multiple revenue streams of the mechanic.

I am a big believer in eliminating the use of additional labor. Why create a job that is not needed, merely to pay for someone to operate a function that technology can solve? This is why grocery stores started to go to automatic self-check-out. It eliminates the waste of clerks to check out customers and reduces the amount of time each customer has to stand in line, while some older customer decides to "shoot the breeze" with a clerk checking them out. If customers want to pay more for an on-call therapist at their local grocery store, maybe that's an ancillary in itself. But that is doubtful. Technology removes the idea of spending beyond a higher labor rate of pay that the customer, not the business owner, refuses to pay. Customers tend to complain about the cost of things going up, yet they ignore payroll tax and B&O tax increases, that are essentially passed onto them.

Plus, when there are downturns, you do not have to lay someone off who didn't deserve it because customers were no longer buying. When you lay 1 person off, you aren't merely causing financial distress or effecting one person: There might be 2-3 people in the house. There might be a child who can no longer play sports, go on field trips or simply eat enough for proper nutrition. There might be a special needs person or an elderly person living with them in that household. And even if it's a person who is single that you are laying off, that affects various other community members around them. You also do not realize the impact that having a job has when that person you've decided to lay off is not an entrepreneur or does not have financial security. So, reducing the initial need for anyone to be hired, when the role of labor might be in question in the first place, is the smartest move that you can make.

Often people starting businesses hire others and quit their own jobs. Because they want to be in charge. They want to establish themselves. They also do not want to work for anyone. That includes working for themselves. These are the most dangerous, reckless entrepreneurs because they believe their money makes their investment all about an "easy street" life. They will continue to have the same bills, have the same lifestyle that they had while working for others, yet now, without the overall revenue stream to sustain it. With entrepreneurism and quitting your job while also not working at that investment, you are creating many more mouths that need to be fed. And with all of those many more mouths, you are requiring a young new business to sustain your lifestyle, as well as its own operation, without any hiccups or fluctuations in the marketplace. That is a unicorn business model if there has ever been one. And unicorns aren't real nor should they be taken as fact, sight unseen, as existing.

I would also recommend understanding that the more children that you have, the less likely you are to sustain a new business independent of your own current source of income. There are some examples where, when your back is to the wall, you can do anything regardless of having a child or three children. And even if you are a single parent with no sources of child support from the other half. But that also speaks to desperation. You aren't going to pay anyone to work the new endeavor, you will do it yourself, lose sleep, lose hours with your children, and sometimes, not see them at all. You have to be cognizant of the fact that there are only so many units of time during the waking hours of daylight. Sure, you may keep your regular job, but if you do have to spread the peanut butter a bit thinner by using up more units of time that would normally be spent at home, or sleeping, exchanging those units for the ability to operate your own business, just realize the cost. Sometimes, this is how kingmakers are established. J.K. Rowling was a single mom, utilizing government assistance, who wrote in her spare time. Things like this can happen, however, the "yes, but..." guy on your shoulder may also talk you out of it.

This is where the conversation of compound interest arrives. You may have taken a finance class, understanding that if you had saved $200 over 30 years ago, it would be over $1,300 today. Some of the compound interest talk features you gaining a 5% interest rate, and just sitting on your duff while it collects. And while $1,300 over 30 years doesn't sound like a lot out of $200, it is really the entire measurement of time that does mean a lot. Imagine all of that candy machine money, net not gross, that was stuffed away into a savings account. You just let it sit there. You did the dirty work, you didn't spend it on anything, and you decided to not stand in the way of compound interest. Remember, these are non-labor inducing items. Twenty hours of your time a month, likely divided by 2.5 hours each Saturday and Sunday, servicing candy machines, then putting the money into a savings account and forgetting about it. This is where small business exists for a reason. The measurement of time rather than the expenditure of flash. Too often, people want to take what they've earned and spend it on a Cadillac Escalade. Instead, focus on earning $30,000 gross, gaining about $25,000 net, and just letting it sit in a true savings account, compounding interest.

There is a mentality at play here. Some of it has to do with the idea that you will save more than you will spend. Another component is asking yourself whether it is smarter to initiate retail or a business that requires a wider amount of service time by you, rather than simply being a great saver. Too few times are we presented with the ultimatum that we are merely attempting to not work a job for someone else, and we aren't really too keen at working at all. Thus we create barriers that will circumvent the overall problem: We don't really want to save to build up a million dollars. We merely want to spend a million dollars. Or more. And this is why people are often in credit card and other debt, beyond their means. They aren't attempting to build anything. They are merely spending their way into new debt holes that they cannot pull themselves out of.

This book is actually a measure of compound interest within the idea of ancillary income. It cost me nothing to write. I jotted down notes throughout the past few years, I taught several business classes, engaged with students, in a paid opportunity with a university. So, I've workshopped out the conversations that I am having with you. Then, I took several units of time, over the course of a few years, and wrote in those small periods. Then I let the various word documents sit on a hard drive, didn't die or lose eyesight or motor function during that period, and rewrote all of the documents while on a paid 2024 Winter Break. Then I emailed everything off to my proofreader, who ensured that my text was solid, paid a small fee for that, then paid for a book cover, and then compiled the book together with Adobe InDesign, lastly uploaded everything to Amazon, which took care of the marketing, etc.

Within a year, I will have broken-even on this Business Book investment because of the royalty structure, and I know how many total paperbacks, audio books or kindle books that I have to sell on

Amazon. Within a few years, I will have yielded a small, but nice profit that will insert itself automatically into my bank account yielding a 5% interest rate. The first time that I did this was in 2008, where I wrote The Sportscasters Notebook, when Amazon's book publishing service was brand new. Over that 16 year period, I generated over $12,000 on a book that cost me $100 to write and have edited. The original cover was black with white lettering. The magic of compound interest, in this small business form, was that I didn't continue to think about it. Once the book was up in the marketplace, it regenerated as many books as needed, Amazon got its cut, I got my royalty, and it averaged $750 annually in book sales. I recognize that the "yes, but..." guy on my shoulder would like to remind me that $750 isn't a lot of money. But the risk-tasker on my other shoulder shouts over the "yes, but..." guy, reminding him and me that the money is generated without me having to do anything that year to achieve it. The $750 average simply wills itself into existence after a while. Who am I to stand in the way of this compound interest? I would be a fool to do so.

And that $750 has now served as floater money for me to write and produce other books. Some fiction. Some nonfiction. All that carry with them their own sources of royalty. Every year, more royalties compound, save into an account, or get uploaded into a Roth IRA that buys S&P 500 shares. Nothing is built within a silo. Everything helps generate more. I have never been married, never bought a house, had children, nor been through a divorce. Things that often wipe people out, cause them to restart over, and place themselves in financial situations that are untenable. I am not suggesting that everyone has the same ease to do things either. However, let me get on my soapbox for a moment: One of the issues lately in this country, is the idea that everyone should be as slow as the dumbest, most idiotic person on the planet. Unless you have various mental or physical barriers, and sometimes if you do, you should hold yourself to a higher standard. If that means merely saving money rather than spending every dime of it, that matters. Otherwise, you are playing to the chorus of someone else's misfortune as your own, expecting everyone to feel sorry for you as well, which they don't.

Understand that developing your playbook means doing things that are a bit out of the norm. I film all of my classes for the students, with the A.I. 4k camera on myself. I also attach a wireless non-amplified lapel microphone, combining the audio and video into one video file for a private YouTube link for my students. If they miss a class, they can refer back to the lecture. However, I also retain all of these videos. All three years of lecturing in seven classes. And I always have the ability, since I am the only one shown in the lectures, to use these classes for my own independent online courses, where I can receive ancillary revenue itself. I haven't done that yet, but you never know. Opportunities to receive more ancillaries, not less, is always around the corner.

When you think about units of time, you have to think about the output as well as the input. Yes, you are inputting several things during specific units of time. But this time is not being robbed from you. It is throwaway time, sitting in an office or somewhere else, that you basically let drift off without a fight anyway. So, why not craft that small unit of time into something useful. We are talking about your specific break time from work; in the majority of states, you are provided with two fifteen minute breaks per eight hours. And with remote work, those units of time can be larger. If you are expected to do a core job, and you do that job, and finish with more time available to you, why are you working harder for someone else's gain? They aren't going to pay you additionally beyond what your work entails. The idea of getting a promotion or raise is rather ridiculous as COVID-19's pandemic proved. Jobs working for others do not gain for you the amount of income that you desire. Only producing your own goods will do that. Gold watches are great, but they are also cheap. And everyone who is in a position of authority, who is younger than you, believes that you are an obstacle to whatever their goal is as well.

Now, let's really talk about the bigger issue with units of time. The amount of interest you are giving away daily through credit cards and other means of financial destruction. This is where you are leveraging yourself into a greater debt, simply to have things that impress people that you will never really engage or meet with. Great, you have a bigger truck. Now you carry with it a lot more debt load along with interest. Same with a giant house. This is part of the bigger conundrum. The financial institution that you want a loan from will not provide it to you, without a house, without a source of income from a W2 (i.e. by working for someone else). And this creates the larger chasm: You basically have to go into debt, have a job working for someone else, along with some property that can be leveraged, in order to gain a small business loan from a financial institution.

Financial institutions are not stupid organizations. They realize that this is a weird paradox, but they do not care. They want your money, they want your property and resources. And they do not expect your small business to pan out. Keep having those great business plans. But once you hit the street and truly learn who your customer is and is not, your business plan is essentially worthless. To a bank, they want the safest bet possible. And the applicant pays the price by having to borrow too much money, without understanding the scope of the small business problem from the beginning.

And this is where a small business loan is stupid. Because you see the large amount of money being placed into your account. You think everything is fine. Then the hemorrhage of cash flowing out, instead of in, begins. You will spend a ton of money up-front, especially if you gain it in a loan, because you won't see it as valued as something that you are budget-conscious about in the beginning. So, instead of being the tightest with money, you become the loosest. The other issue is the amount of non-profits and other community groups that will suddenly seek you out to donate to their fundraiser or cause. For the first few years, you need to deny all of these requests. Make up whatever excuse you need to. You need to stay in business, not give away the store. A lot of people in certain areas such as non-profits are paid in order to fundraise for their own salaries, where 95% of the money goes toward administrative overhead. When they claim it goes to the community, it really goes to them. You have to be tough, you have to be rigid and dogmatic. Otherwise, you will be out of business entirely.

EMERGING IDEAS

Ideas are everywhere. And they are nowhere. You cannot manufacture a successful idea without a problem to which you can solve. This concept evades a lot of people. They simply want a business, therefore, why shouldn't you buy from them? That doesn't work unless you offer a solution that the consumer can latch onto which solves their problem. And the public is fickle about what solves their problems. Sometimes, they do not even recognize that they have a problem at all, until you present a solution which makes the problem glaringly obvious. Therein lies the rub: Being able to present a solution no one knows that they can fix with a problem, until after you've already invested in figuring out what the problem is in the first place.

I met a man in the 1990s who started a window cleaning business with a squeegee and a spray bottle. He had been laid off from his job with his wife divorcing him. In short, he had little capital to start a business. But as he looked at his neighbor's houses, he noticed their dirty windows. All of them, were absolutely filthy. He told me that he went to the Dollar Store, the cheapest place he could find what he needed. The man invested $1.59 in a squeegee and spray bottle as a two-for-one combo deal, then walked around his neighborhood, offering his services. Within a few days, he had generated $500. Within a month, he was already hiring another window washer to go to the nearby neighborhoods. And within six months, he had taken over contracts of one-story office buildings. From a $1.59 investment, the man had created an empire.

We tend to over-think what is needed in order to survive. This comes in the form of requiring a space in the mall, or enough overhead products to generate revenue as we see fit. But everything good often starts small. Very small. Do not mistake the tech bro bubbles of investment, where they tend to do massive fundraising rounds. Those are on the luxury side of selling dreams that often do not sustain themselves long-term. Small businesses begin small because the people starting them have little capital to invest. But they have a solution to a problem. Often a problem that the public didn't realize it had to begin with.

And that is how small business start-ups are made. People confound what they need to start a small business, which overwhelms them completely. We tend to view locations as major achievements instead of what they actually yield in actual net revenue. Take the shopping mall for example. It holds a strange place of value for your business to be located in a shopping mall, despite the exorbitantly high price-per-square-foot lease prices of their stores. And the fact that shopping malls have had a downturn in overall foot traffic since the 1990s, minus the three-week madhouse of the Christmas shopping season. It does not make sense for an alterations store to be housed in a shopping mall, even if the lease is free, given the mall's store hour requirements. An alternations store is likely going to experience less customers who are seeking a tuxedo or bridal gown adjustment, compared to the wandering herd of poorly dressed t-shirt and denim jeans set that makes its way through the concourse. Knowing your audience is key to knowing whether you fit into a certain location. That is why rich, fatty foods do well in a shopping mall food court, and health food does not.

A young realtor named Danielle had a separate small start-up business idea, a clothing outfit, which she presented to the nearby shopping mall. This occurred in 2018 and the shopping mall was looking for new, local tenants. The shopping mall's agreement would have the owner receive a "next-to-nothing" lease for a year, to build up the entrepreneur's business. The shopping mall loved the idea, because Danielle had a proven track record of pop-up fair and Internet sales with her clothing line. In short, she had a following. The shopping mall gave her a great deal on leasing a space, less than a fraction of what they normally would require. It was $100 a month which doesn't even pay for electricity. There was only one issue with the space: The mall required Danielle's business to be open from 9 a.m. to 9 p.m. daily, Monday thru Sunday.

It didn't take long for Danielle to realize that the shopping mall lease was untenable for her. The amount of labor hours paid to staff simply to keep the business open, compared to the actual foot traffic, did not pencil out. Keep in mind that in Washington State in 2019 when the store opened was $13.50 - that meant Danielle was paying $15.19 per labor hour after figuring in payroll taxes. One 13 hour shift (two employees total) would mean $197.47 in labor overhead alone. Every seven days, that amount in labor hours would equal $1,382.29. And within a month, that meant $5,529.16 in labor cost overhead, without factoring in product supplies or the mall lease. Danielle opted out of her mall lease within three months, found a warehouse space, and opened the store on her terms, limiting staff overhead completely. In short, Danielle figured out that what she thought she needed - a mall space - was actually a detriment to her small businesses' survival.

People hate math. Some will tell you that for them, math is a disability. Mainly, math is an inconvenient truth. The general public does not concern themselves with the taxation or overhead costs that a business pays. Because the general public does not equate the business being served with taxation or overhead as part of the product price that the general public will end up paying. The general public thinks that the cost isn't passed on from a business to them. All they see is the end retail price of the product, then complain about prices going up. If you asked to see their voting record, those complaining would likely be defensive despite voting for the pro-tax politicians and pro-sales tax initiatives on the ballot.

The general public likes to lull themselves asleep at the costs they charge themselves, then jump wide awake after they get charged. The Business & Occupation (B&O) tax is a way for municipalities to pass on a tax to the consumer, thru local businesses, without the consumer getting upset about it. The B&O tax pays for a multitude of public services. And it charges businesses based on gross sales. Businesses then calculate their B&O taxes into their cost of goods (COGS), then raise their prices accordingly, in order to maintain their profit margins. As an entrepreneur with a solution to a problem, this may seem strange for you to think about the taxation or labor hours that you will pay. However, it all matters when calculating whether you have a business at all.

When I took over Charlie's Safari in May 2019, I asked to see the COGs. And within a month, I asked the store manager, Ashley, if I could see the employee work schedule to calculate out labor ratios. I did this on a Saturday night. Without any warning, half of the staff provided their immediate notice. What I came to discover was that the staff scheduled themselves together at hours when work was light, but they all were able to collect large paychecks. The labor ratios were 135% above revenue, meaning that we were paying for too many staff to stand around, chat with each other, and avoid having to work at all. Then, it got interesting.

Ashley had previously warned me about a young person at the family fun center that she wanted to fire. That young woman's name was Alexis, who looked tuned out, bored and didn't follow any standards at all. The night of the great exodus, however, Alexis didn't provide her notice. I looked on the security monitors, seeing Alexis filling out cashiers slips for the nightly drop. It looked like she was crying. She cared about the place and had been working there for years. She simply wasn't part of Ashley's clique, therefore, Ashley saw her as useless. I met with Alexis the next morning, we had a great conversation, and within a few months, Alexis was operating the store as a manager. She listened, fully engaged, and kept the labor ratios at 24% against weekly revenue. Alexis likened the process of the work schedule to Jenga.

Once I had Alexis brought in, she became invested. This is the magic of owning a small business. You have the ability to change lives and mentor others. In state government, you are held to positional duties, raises and other factors. But small business allows you to pivot, move quick, and reward those who deserve it. Alexis definitely deserved everything she got. From the withdrawn young employee to someone who directed others, Alexis handled herself well. Because she didn't hate math and understood what I was trying to do with labor ratios. And with any startup, beyond the idea stage, comes the harsh reality of what you are getting into.

The lack of basic business mathematics for the general consumer is not reserved solely for labor ratios. It also pertains to any component of business operation in general. Until they are doing it themselves, there are few if any general consumers who understand what it takes to operate a functional small business. They will provide advice without consideration, but that comes with the territory. This phenomenon is not reserved solely for business either. The general consumer has become divorced from many things, including where its food comes from and how it is made. Ask any city dweller about farming or agriculture, most cannot tell you where their food comes from or how it arrived there. If left to their own devices tomorrow, with all of the grocery stores shut down entirely, none of them could grow enough plants to survive, let alone thrive. They wouldn't know how. It would be foreign to them. Especially if the Internet shut down as they would have no place to look it up anyway.

Even with the Internet, the majority of general consumers do not look up the details. They do not research information despite the history of the world's knowledge at their fingertips. This is the divorcing of convenience. The majority of young people, despite several years of taking history classes throughout the U.S. educational system, could not provide details of World War II or Viet Nam or anything generally. The response commonly provided is: "I wasn't born yet." Turn off the electricity for a week or month, watch how quickly society relying on electricity crumbles. And how quickly, areas where electricity or the Internet isn't as available thrive. This is the issue with divorcing yourself from any subject. You feel too confident to know how to act on something, without actually having the skillset available to actually act on something if the time came.

This is why the majority of start-up small businesses fail. Not from a lack of trying. But because of a lack of knowledge. A lack of research. A removal of developing that business over time while working for someone else. Much like knowing details of history, if it is deemed inconvenient to know, then it is difficult to muster up the strength to know it. Business appears as simple as can be. Spend a dollar, make two dollars. What could be hard about that? Except for the details. The mired inability to research in advance on whether your business has merit or not.

THE "YES, BUT..." GUY ON YOUR SHOULDER

Whether you recognize it or not, as an entrepreneur, you have on each of your shoulders, a small person whispering in your ear. And no, they are not the angel and the devil. You wish. Instead, you have the risk-taker who tells you to go for it, and a "yes, but..." guy who gives you every reason under the sun what can go wrong if you do. This can be maddening if you are intending to be an entrepreneur. The "yes, but..." guy always has arguments, and sometimes, is working against your better judgement. And yet, that "yes, but..." guy is always ready to talk you out of something, anything, because it would be too risky otherwise.

Don't get me wrong. The "yes, but..." guy is not evil. That little person sitting on your shoulder just doesn't want you to get hurt. This can happen in other instances as well, such as dating, but you have to be aware of what listening to the "yes, but..." guy will do to you. You will also see that little person sitting on the shoulder of other people, who are interested in developing their own empire. You won't see the person per se, but more figuratively, in other people's eyes. Especially when you suggest things in an attempt to help them with their entrepreneurial issues. Sometimes, this also takes the form of their own verbal challenges back to you, when you state a problem, and they utter things like "well, that's how things work," or "it's like that everywhere." These types of negative cofounding comments shut down intellectual stimulation and conversation, rather than create more of it.

Much like how conversation is devolved to the point to where we cannot decipher between true sexism and random comment. This title would be a good example. I could use the term "gal" or "woman" or whatever. And someone will be upset that I didn't. Because they truly cannot comprehend the overall subject matter, thus they get stuck on something that they can control. Such as using the term "guy" which is obviously a cis-gender term established of the patriarchy meant to hold them down. In some ways, I am being unintentionally intentional. Mainly because if this is what you want to focus on, you paid for the book, you can now toss it into the trash or firepit, because I got my royalty and we can always print others. When you focus on the silliness of something unintentional, you stop focusing on what matters, and you stop becoming an entrepreneur. Instead, you become an activist, which is something that is railing against something, thus forgetting about their customer altogether for the greater good.

That "yes, but..." guy wants you to think about that nonsense. Mainly because it divorces themselves, and yourself, from the greater good of knowing how to sell or do something. I dealt with a coffee roaster a few years ago, who was selling his coffee out of mobile trailers, but refused to go into Starbucks to look at their environment. Despite readying the launch of his first retail coffee shop. His "yes, but..." guy mentality had hindered him useless against the idea that Starbucks Coffee might know what they are doing. Because, well, they aren't hip, or cool, or whatever he is. When I meet people resistant to the idea of understanding what their large competitors are doing, I see that "yes, but..." guy dancing in their eyes, talking in their ears, refusing the notion that the big seller who has spent millions on their brand, would have any idea how to operate their business.

Don't get me wrong, there are ways to combat and win against the big competitor. Namely, that you have to be willing to do various things that the big competitor cannot do. There are only a few brands of coffee sold by Starbucks. They cannot carry all of them, completely, in each of their 41,000+ stores. Impossible. Thus, there is a hole in their system to exploit. You will not reach the same type of volume or sales that Starbucks Coffee has, but you can see where the holes are, if you go into a few Starbucks Coffee stores, look around, and examine. You have to tune down the "yes, but..." guy for a bit, and ask your risk-taking person on your other shoulder, what they would be doing. Chances are, within a few minutes at each Starbucks Coffee location, the risk-taker will point it out to you. Funny how that occurs.

Starbucks Coffee is not simply about selling coffee. It is about selling an experience. And selling ancillaries. A lot of folks scoff at the last statement, until you see where their profit margins are. They tend to be in the coffee mugs, t-shirts and other items that are laid out around the stores. Ancillaries do not expire. Well, some do, such as food items or bottled drinks, which are not something that you associate Starbucks Coffee with. But those ancillaries are still a part of the overall experience. Same with gift cards, which tend to hold more lost credit by the customer, therefore become a greater profit margin for Starbucks Coffee itself. All of these are things that your risk-taker will notice. The "yes, but..." guy on your other shoulder will suggest otherwise or challenge it as an opportunity that you need to initiate on.

So, let's take down Starbucks Coffee where they cannot compete. Experience to the maximum level. If Starbucks Coffee can only offer a few coffee beans, why can't we offer more? I suggested this to that local coffee roaster. And you could see the "yes, but..." guy on his shoulder stop the conversation. You could see it in the roaster's eyes. People wear a lot of their negativity in their eyes. Whether it be jealousy or lack of ambition, the eyes as the windows to the soul is a metaphor that exists for a reason. The roaster shot back with there are only 7 countries that make coffee beans, so my suggestion was idiotic. I asked Google on my smart phone. Turns out that there are 79 countries which do coffee beans. The coffee roaster was surprised, but the "yes, but..." guy decided to speak up again, saying that it would cost too much, requiring too much inventory, in order to carry 79 different countries worth of coffee beans.

And this is where I ask the question: "But what if you did???"

This is similar to the question asked by Leslie Chow in The Hangover films: "But did you die?" Basically, you can be upset that something happened, but you lived through the experience, so shut up and tell yourself that you survived. That to me is a great message. People can act decisive or put-upon. Depends on who they actually are intending to be. And if you didn't die, you survived to tell the tale, well, everything you are stating right now is nothing more than a shabby complaint. Therefore, shut up and move forward. Keep moving forward.

The coffee roaster can come up with any reason why not to do it. Maybe it is cost of inventory, or just products with expiration dates. Unroasted coffee beans can last up to 12 months according to Google. Perhaps even longer if you shrink wrap them. And imagine if you did carry 25 different countries' coffee beans. You make it an experience where customers could venture into a section of your shop, select different roasting packages, and you could charge far more than average. People do not know how much something costs as much as they think they do. And the amount of availability, shipping time, and other issues change the conversation entirely. Because they want it... now. This is the key toward the experience: Either I can wait until it is sent to me, if I trust the online vendor to do so, or it's in my hands because I paid the price of buying locally. It all depends. As does word of mouth. And envy. And keeping up with the Joneses. Which is part of retail experiences. If the Joneses have it, whyca n't I have it, right now? I'm not even sure that I will like it, but if the Joneses have it, then I should have it too. Otherwise, it would be downright foolish to avoid doing the same thing that everyone else is getting to experience. This is how you get a line around the block for your product.

Go to Voodoo Donuts in Portland, Oregon. There is a line. These are just donuts. But go to any Krispy Kreme Donuts, which is franchised out. There is a line there too. Lines exist when people think that you have a product they have to be a part of. They likely do not need the donut. But they want the donut. They have to have the donut. Fear Of Missing Out = F.O.M.O. While this has been categorized as an Internet trend, it has been a part of retail forever. When supplies run low, suddenly everyone comes to buy. Look at how Black Friday sales prior to the 2020 Pandemic were notorious for fist fights for products found throughout the year at a higher supply volume. Now, there's urgency. There's demand. There's insanity on how to react.

Customer experience is about eliciting something that they cannot get anywhere else for their time. Browsing is great. It means that they are looking, thinking. So, great, you have 25 varieties of coffee beans from parts of the world unknown. All at various prices. What does the showroom area look like? How does it feel? What does it smell like? Everything is about presentation. You can either be a Target store and look like everywhere else, or you can feel like something greater. This comes back to your customer, and what they expect. Imagine that you created a special showroom just for the beans themselves. Something that was away from the rest of the riffraff. It wasn't available to simply everyone, but only those customers "in the know" who are members.

They get alerts on their phone when coffee bean selections come in. They are the first to be part of the new experience. This is where you drive demand. There is a focal point of getting on that membership list, getting to be a part of the action, that causes people to act. They will form the line for you. They will wait to be first, before they become last.

Notice the presentation. The graphic design. Color schemes. Everything tells a story that dances you along the lines of entertaining you. It brings out imagination. Maybe there are coffee beans that taste like vanilla, orange or blueberry. Each of the bags should represent these colors along with the placement on the shelf. But it is more than that. Your employees and yourself need to be true savants on these coffee beans. This is where Starbucks Coffee lacks. Because they have stretched to 41,000+ stores with about 600,000 frontline employees. They have to train their staff on the minimal amount of interest in coffee, in order to drive those sales. By being small and nimble, a smaller coffee retail shop with 25+ different coffee beans can become the corner bookstore. You walk in, weeks after your last visit, and the owner knows your name, brings you aside, and says "I have something you HAVE to try." This means a lot. It is not just taste profiling, but customer appreciation. Be damned the cost of the retail product, it will be bought because "I know a guy."

So, you've got all of these different varieties of coffee beans and a coffee shop. What are your special moments like? Are you looking at having roasters' mornings, with twelve people total in the shop, doors closed, open sign off, in order to fully taste a coffee blend? Imagine how many people would absolutely kill for this experience on a Saturday or Sunday morning. A 6 a.m. moment when no one else is around, suddenly tasting something different, complex. Each of those people being the first to try a new bean from Russia or Ethiopia or San

Clemente. They would get to take a roasted packet home with them as part of the experiential sale, which would include different espresso blends with flavoring, etc. Ideas that help foster new experiences at home, beyond your shop. And beyond the price paid for the experience, you request that they review it with a photograph or video on their social media. Simply to tell everyone else what they think of the coffee beans, and whether it is worth trying. Chances are, you will have a line around the block for that limited addition coffee bean blend by 10 a.m. that same day.

Selection is marketing. Variety is marketing. This idea that branding is merely words or colors is ridiculous. Experiential marketing is taste, flavor, smell. It is "knowing a guy" who works their local coffee shop, walks you through your "coffee journey." That last line is actually not mine. It came from a customer of mine, when I owned The Cider Barrel in downtown Olympia, Washington. Having over 300 hard ciders to choose from, understanding taste profiles was amazing. And the customer told me, " This is all about walking me along my cider journey." I told him that I liked that. A few years later, I told him how other customers had responded with an affirmative nod every time I mentioned the "cider journey." Customers like appreciation of their input as much as anything else you can do for them.

Half empty shelves matter. They place the customer on notice. If you do not buy, someone else will, and you will miss out. When you look at a coin candy machine dispenser, the worst thing you can do is fill every container up to the top. They need to have uneven levels. Human psychology provokes interest when some containers are less than others. That feeds into the idea of demand. The structure of seeing something almost gone creates an impulse. Obviously, it is good, otherwise it would be full like the others. This is how you can also get high volume sales of high margin product. Only place half of the product out for sale. The customer will pick it, much like when they drive through a parking lot, they park next to another car, even if the rest of the lot is empty. Humans gravitate toward each other, and they buy what other people are buying, because it means they are less likely to make a wrong or negative choice that might be criticized. This is why before Lewis & Clark, few people traveled into the Pacific Northwest and there were wild stories about what went on there. After Lewis & Clark's two year expedition ended in 1806, less than 30 years later, in 1832, there were wagon expeditions set to conquer the terrain. Pioneers are often alone. But after they innovate, a tidal wave of interest follows. This is why a roaster having private hours for new coffee bean tasters would help push others to try the same offerings.

This is where the "yes, but..." guy needs to be muzzled. Think of all of the possibilities of brainstorming that are stopped by this little fella sitting on your shoulder. Even if you do not do them, you should consider and weigh them. The problem is, the "yes, but..." guy doesn't even allow you to get the conversation started. Kills the idea right before it comes out of the chute. Stabs it right in the heart with a pencil and breaks it off for good measure. If you cannot play at all in the world of fantasy, you lead a boring life of regret. If you are looking for who that quote came from, well, I wrote it, just now. Because I allowed myself the ability to generate the possibility that I might be able to write something wild, alluring, etc. The difficulty with conditioned people, namely those who have worked state jobs or continual jobs for long periods of time with the same company, is that they reduce their overall risk. And by doing so, they eliminate the idea of actually fostering imagination. When you do that, you kill a little of yourself trying to murder the idea as it comes out the chute.

This is not to say that every idea is completely solid or should be used. But it should be weighed and considered. And you should look at various angles, without the "yes, but..." guy stopping you before the idea fully forms. At least let it germinate. Is there harm in that? I have zero clue why, but to some people, simply having the idea alone is considered a form of destruction and harm. As if having the idea means that it is somehow realized in the ether, therefore dangerous, and could disrupt everything. This is why people come from work, sit in front of the computer or television, and zone out. Prefer not to think about things. It is better that way. Less risky. Until the day that they get laid off, or retire, then find themselves without a source of income or simply bored out of their mind. That's my theory on how all of those senior citizen walking groups got started in the malls. They were bored out of their mind at 6 a.m., then ventured over to the mall which opened at 8 a.m. daily, despite the mall stores not opening until 10 a.m. daily. You do the math. There's a reason for everything. Often, bored is a large component of why people do the things that they do.

And for some reason, people play favor to the "yes, but..." guy as if that little fella on their shoulder is helping them out. Well, at least, it's not the risk-taker, the one that could get them in trouble. See, that's the rub. Without risk, there is no real reward. But with risk, there's the ability to lose. So people would rather not do anything at all. Then claim that they could have done it. Like those who did listen to the risk-taker. But the first group of people didn't. So they have nothing to show for their entire lack of efforts, but bragging rights that they could have done something. See how insidious this line of thinking is? It's cyclical and harmful. Yet, people play this charade constantly. Endlessly. Thinking that they've accomplished something, when clearly they have not.

THE W2 FORM LURE

When you size people up, they come in two forms: Those who require a W2 from someone else, and those who cannot handle a W2 from someone else. I prefer to be in the middle. Why not have some security, while at the same time, innovate while someone else takes the majority of the risk? How does that work? Often, it helps to have the ability to work additional hours at someone else's luxury. You still do the work for them, but you also carve out small instances that help you succeed and move forward. What does that mean? Every moment spent at an office does not denote work produced. And there's no reason you cannot do small little micro things in order to help your own bottom line, while avoiding taking 100-percent risk on your endeavor.

Let's create a $100 business cost scenario that you can do, while working an office job. Become a notary public. For $100, you can have the licensing application to your state, as well as the insurance coverage. You get yourself listed on the licensing websites for an additional $100 annually. Then you figure out what people are charging, and you charge accordingly. So, here's the rub: Do this while doing your office job. It is a way to bring in extra income while not relying 100-percent on it. How do you perform notary public functions while at an office job? Somewhere, there is a lobby, or an off-site coffee shop nearby. Have your own website, your own automatic scheduler, take a 30 minute break from your office job, then perform the notary functions. Chances are, within that 30 minute window, you will earn more in that time than you will for the eight hours at the office job. And you have not committed any act of negligence as you took off the time at the office job to perform the task at hand.

There are small micro gigs that supplement the overall lifestyle operation. And you can retain your W2 from some other employer. I am merely presenting this as an option, because there are some naysayers out there who will prevent you from attempting to go independent, and start your own small business. That comes back to the risk-taker on your shoulder being muzzled in favor of the "yes, but..." guy on your other shoulder. Funny how we often listen to the bad advice, merely because it is presented as an opinion of safety, rather than a fair assessment of what we should be doing. So, if you require a W2 to survive, this is one way to do it. Remember, that your office job is merely temporary. Even if you work at it for 10-to-20-to-30 years, it will be terminated when the business or state decides to reduce labor force. So if you have additional income streams, it will help in the long run, regardless of how long you do it before your job is eliminated, or they decide to "retire you out."

I recognize that I presented a dark picture. Someone who worked at their job for 30 years is reduced to being either retired out or laid off because someone decided their position was no long relevant. But be honest with yourself. Take that quick assessment. Are you really in a safe position with any job? Whether it be a state job or at a large corporation? You are merely there until you are not there. Until someone decides that they can either do without you, or reduce your position to eliminate the amount of salary they are paying you. Whether you choose to retire on your own terms or not. And then you wake up one day, shocked that you are no longer employed, and you have bills to pay. Over 80 percent of divorces are initiated by women, after men lose their jobs. Mainly because breadwinning jobs performed by women often have them questioning why they need a man around in the first place. Either be mad with that statement or ignore it but understand that the reality of you losing that "safe" W2 job is just as credible as not succeeding at your entrepreneurial one.

The majority of successful entrepreneurs have burnt fingertips. Both literally and figuratively. They are not the types who looked at having a "roach coach" food truck and thought it would be fashionable to own. They understood that they were committing to working themselves inside a metal box for many hours of labor, which may or may not yield out what they initially invested in. That's how fingertips get burned. Those that commit are often too stubborn to quit, and sometimes, they still fail. But at least they were fully committed to the overall process and understanding of what they were trying to do. When you are merely pulling effort as a W2 employee for someone else's business, or as a state worker, you do not understand all of the machinations that go into that operation. Because you do not have to. You are not risking anything, therefore you do not see where the burned fingertips occur. Or how close to the edge of the razor that the business is from failing.

This is one of my criticisms (of many) that I have for elected officials. Many of them pass along taxation, permit fees and other expenses to small businesses, without risking anything themselves. They do not see the damage, only treating the end-result as an endless flow of tax revenue for their projects at the city, county and state level. Federal is another animal altogether. If there is anything that will make you a hardcore anti-tax advocate, who is willing to lose "friends" on social media or in your social groups, it will be owning your own business. Because once you spot all of the taxes, permit fees, approval delays, etc. that you have to endure, chances are that you will be so anti-tax that your social circle will be reduced. The people who do not own businesses, who typically support public projects or shrug off taxation concerns, will eliminate themselves from your life. They will self-select out because you are heartless or uncaring. And because they do not comprehend the issue. Everyone loves a tax that they do not pay, everyone loves a discount only they get.

For all those out there willing to work for a W2, they tend to forget the amount of time spent on a cover letter and resume, along with the interview process, the worry and anxiety of how they did in front of people, and whether they will be able to do the task at hand. Then they sit at a job, earning a 2-to-5 percent raise bi-annually, and think that they could earn more if they just apply for another job down the street. To another company. To go through the entire process again. Some of this mindset also works within the concept of business creation. Simply having a business is not enough. You have to be willing to develop a business in order to sell a business. If you aren't selling the business, you have to put more revenue into the business, with the hopes of growing the business. That also means taking on whatever taxation or permit fees are applied by the elected officials who think that you are a greedy C.E.O. and have convinced the voters that you are a piggy bank meant to be cracked open just a little bit more.

I am always fascinated by the idea that people are willing to do lower finance jobs, but unwilling to also do some side business performing standard accountant duties. Imagine the money that they could charge their neighbors, if they have a finance job, simply by doing annual taxes. Especially if it is a local business owner, who's willing to spend a lot of money in order to not think about the taxation or bookkeeping. Yet, you will see these lower finance jobs (such as a bank teller or bank manager), who is unwilling to do whatever certification and insurance is required, in order to perform the bookkeeping duties. With technology such as customer relationship management (C.R.M.) software, all of these items can be downloaded into an accounting software that does most of the work for the bookkeeper remotely. Then it comes down to filing quarterly and other taxes, as well as access to specific bank accounts to withdraw from. This creates a small business for the finance person, that increases their own cash flow and savings, and potentially builds more revenue than the eventual 2-to-5 percent raise they are supposedly expecting from their employer. Jumping from employer to employer has its own opportunity costs as well, mainly from the time you are willing to spend going through the application to interview to job duty process. It might be better, and more lucrative, to worry less about getting a higher demanding job than a lower demanding job, when you can do additional work without many more hours of labor.

We still think of units of time as labor. Forty hours of labor per week. Then we are put upon, exhausted, never to work more than that. Because we need our space. Time to ourselves, etc. This reduces our overall work enhancement as a young professional. Because we are diluting our energy at a time when we have the most energy, and assessing that working more frequently at different revenue streams is a bad thing. This is where "yes, but..." guy on your shoulder shares their space with a "put-upon" cousin. This "put-upon" cousin is smaller, but sometimes gets in your ear with a loud enough voice, telling you not to do more. Because, well, that's really something that puts upon you extra effort and you do not have the energy to do so.

When teaching at a university, I have encountered a lot of students who are talked out of opportunities by that "put-upon" cousin on their shoulder. Internships. Networking opportunities. Various methods of growing their own ability to broaden their experiences and their job prospects. That "put-upon" cousin will talk all day long, getting that student to remove themselves from opportunity consideration. Why work harder when others aren't? This is the rub about being at a university for four years as a student. You have various opportunities to network, build and intern. You can make the most of those opportunities, engage with folks in different office or prospective work environments, and emerge with more experience than your graduating counterparts. Yet, young people listen to that "put-upon" cousin, sometimes they also listen to downright mentality-ill losers on the Internet, gaining advice from those you wouldn't dare ask anything of. But they don't qualify that advice or who is giving it. And by listening to the worst advice, by doing less when they should be doing more, they end up removing themselves from the most valuable teacher of life, which is experience.

Experience is something that needs to occur individually. The reason that you intern, is that you learn new skills. Sure, you didn't get paid up-front, but that's because you learn the core of the business, when everyone thinks they got one over on you. This is why certain jobs have internships, and certain basic labor jobs do not. Because no one sees themselves interning for free at a basic labor position. But if they did, they would learn more about the position, and be able to do the job on their own, for themselves, without anyone but them owning the business. This comes back to that risk-taker who sits on your shoulder, egging you on. Which is why when people spend time in a university dorm room, they come up with the next Google or tech company. Because they are eliminating several components of overhead, while learning the basics of the job around them.

Risk-taking is also something that is not at certain people's core. Nor is networking. Or when they do networking, they are often the worst at it. Such as when they are required by their boss to network at a Chamber of Commerce luncheon. The worst networkers are the ones who go grab their food when the buffet line opens, then go sit at their table. First, the food is always terrible. Buffet style food at any luncheon is glorified, over-salted, slop. Second, you are paid to meet people, engage and chat. I always go to a meeting without my nametag and go shake hands and say hello to as many folks during that time as possible. I enter the luncheon 30 minutes before the start of the formal meeting, then pull an "Irish Goodbye" right as everyone has sat down and the boring presentation is about to start. None of the information presented is worth a damn at any Chamber of Commerce meeting. The only reason to attend is to get in, see some people, then get out. Whether you pay for the lunch ticket or not will never translate to any business being conducted, which is the whole point in the first place.

My warning in advanced networking is understanding what the purpose of the networking group is. Several of these groups are nothing more than "friend" events. There is little commerce exchanged. Instead, it is a friend support system, often guided with a multi-level marketing (MLM) feel to it. Are they merely you avoiding selling, instead of finding friends? This is no different than a therapist who ends up engaging with a client enough that they don't really resolve issues, instead, they talk like old friends, except one person is paying the other. Some of these networking groups become hostile to the idea of actual commerce. They are about friend-making centers, but also in some ways, large wastes of time, becoming cliquish. Don't let your current boyfriend keep you from your future husband. This statement also arrives in the idea of networking groups that are glorified MLMs, masking as commerce-building.

You also have to learn who to associate with, and who you avoid. Specifically for your own reputation. I had a reckless commercial insurance agent friend who offered up a mess of a personal life. You have to ask yourself whether you want to fully associate with that person once you are in small business for yourself. Fun when you are in your youth is totally different when you are making money for yourself. Customers associate and pair people together. The hard-charging reckless fun of the commercial insurer was something that I eventually had to separate from. Love the guy personally, but there were too many customers that paired both the insurer and myself together, thus his antics became something that I would always have to explain away. Social media does not help in these matters of having private moments stay private. And you can not control where they are spread as well as who sees them.

This creates a conversational touchpoint about networking in general. Every time that you do network, you are likely to do it on someone else's turf. Why? If you can find a space, why not create your own networking event? Do it once a month. Have it at a favorite restaurant on a Tuesday at 11:30 a.m. to 1 p.m. Nothing ever happens at this time, yet it is an opportune time to do something when everyone is usually available. Just network, have a meet-up where local business owners can meet. Maybe you charge $5 or $10 per head, but imagine not putting a lot of effort into it. Just use your social media or an email marketing chain, get people involved, and really start to engage. If you have a tribe of 25 or 50 or 100, it is still a tribe of people. Get them together at a meeting, take some pictures, then set up the next event for the following month. There is never not a need for another networking function which brings in newer people who may not have an opportunity to engage locally otherwise.

This also creates your own home turf. Even if it's not your own turf. Because no restaurant owner in their right mind is going to turn away any business of any kind. Especially on a Tuesday at 11:30 a.m. to 1 p.m., regardless of the area. Whether it's in Smallville U.S.A. or Metropolis, there is never going to be a time when every Tuesday is booked, and where people showing up, with the ability to purchase their own meals and drinks, isn't going to be attractive to a restaurant owner with a meeting room. And if there is a restaurant owner with a meeting room who thinks they are going to charge you for the opportunity to engage your networking folks, then move onto the next space. There are plenty of spaces, plenty of restaurants willing to host for free, or should. We have gotten too many inflated egos in the world of business where restaurant owners are forgetting that they are in the service business, not the space rental business.

Back in the summer of 2010, I had a small comedy booking business, called Squeaky's Comedy, in Spokane, Washington. The format was simple: clean comedy. Which really angered all of the local "stand-up comedians" who were foul-mouthed and unfunny. We ran several comedy shows at a local bar called The Red Lion Barbeque, in their back showroom on a Saturday night. They didn't charge us, we didn't charge them, everyone who entered paid a cover, and the business made money on beer and food. We sold out every show at 100 people for a 50 person capacity showroom. Then, after five straight weekends of sold-out shows, the Red Lion owner, George, decided he was going to have to charge us. You know, for the right to book the room. Turns out, despite making $1,500 a night on drink and food service, he wanted an extra $500 to hold the room for us. So, obviously, we moved our shows to a local card room with a larger showroom down the street, shocking George completely.

I recognize that this seems in contradiction to what I told you about the idea of valuing space. Charging for space does matter. However, that is when you aren't reaping ancillaries off of that space as a condition of the activity occurring. For instance, if they didn't have the space to charge the cover, you wouldn't be making money off of the people eating food because they wouldn't be in that space. That is the difference maker right there. There's a wide chasm between charging for space when the activity overhead is entirely covered by one person, rather than it being the guests, who are backing the activity itself.

There is also a difference between the space that you value, and the space that others do not value. You can exploit those who do not recognize the value in their own real estate. A perfect example is that of your local movie theater. Watch for a local movie theater that attempts to "rent out" its theater auditoriums for special events. Nothing says that a local film festival cannot be operated by a for-profit business. Or that you cannot do a call for entries on a "film festival" site. Especially if you give yourself months' worth of lead time in order to do it. Nothing says any of that, because it isn't written anywhere as a rule that what I am suggesting is impossible. If comic conventions can be handled by private entities, so can film festivals, and other events. The movie theater itself is not in the movie showing business anyway. They are there to sell food. And if you can get the theater for a cheap price, if you can get the independent movies for free as a "festival entry" to where the producers actually pay a fee to have it submitted, and if you can get businesses to sponsor the festival, then all you have left is the film festival attendees themselves. Which means selling tickets. And merchandise. And the fact that I have presented this idea to you, when there are thousands of multiplexes throughout the country sitting in near-empty darkness as streaming becomes more popular, makes it a sure bet that if you can take the risk and make the event, there is a large reward for you if there's also a packed house.

The "yes, but..." guy is tapping you on the shoulder. He is pounding on your ear. Of course, he doesn't want you to attempt this. Of course, there is no way that you can make "a go" of any of this. Because, well, there has to be proof of concept. Right? That's how all things work. Proof of concept. Except sometimes you don't see a road, only dirt, and you have to pave it yourself. That's when the real rubber meets the road. Once you pave the road, other folks will start their own versions of their film festival, mainly because you provided them with the road map. Before 1954, no one had accomplished a 4-minute-mile run. Then Roger Bannister set it. Then two months later, John Landy became the second person. The four minute mile barrier has been accomplished by 1,755 athletes as of December 2024. Imagine all of the people prior to Roger Bannister, who claimed that setting the 4-minute-mile run was impossible. Over 3,000 years of naysayers. Then, over 1,755 people within a 70 year mark who have proved them all wrong. That is the proof of concept tidal wave. Once it occurs, everyone sees what is possible, then the impossible becomes totally possible to them as well.

There are always going to be folks who shit on their own shoes. They will ruin a good thing because it wasn't their idea in the first place, therefore they have less investment into it. This occurred when I sold The Cider Barrel, a 300+ cider bar showroom in downtown Olympia, in the summer of 2023. I sold it to a local realtor after generating $200,000 off of a 585-square-foot microbar that was only open less than 20 hours a week. The realtor was shown everything, including how to generate through catering events, and how to really push new varietals out before the stock even hit the shelves. Within a year and a half, she was looking to sell the place, had completely run down the inventory selection from 300+ hard cider options to less than 30, and had transformed the showroom into a Gen-Z hangout.

The issue with her re-format of The Cider Barrel is that she didn't like the original customers who bought from her. These would be the 30-to-45 age women who would show up, buy varieties of 12oz cans in two or three cases, spend $400, then leave within five minutes. They wanted 300+ cans so they were "in the know" and could drink at home with their loved-one or friends, as the center of attention. This is really about understanding and engaging with your customer, who had the means to keep the small showroom afloat. Instead, the new owner of The Cider Barrel wanted to have fun people to hang out with, who were "downtown folk" often with nose rings, tattoos and other piercings, but who didn't have much money to their name. When you have a business, you find your customer, but by finding that customer, you also lose other customers. The goal is to find the customer with the most money to spend on your product, instead of switching them out for the customers who have little money to spend. It was a great concept while it lasted, but for her, it didn't last long, as she went for the wrong customers. This occurs when people also brush off high quality potential spouses for an attractive emotionally unavailable loser. I believe I've just explained the divorce rate and how businesses collapse within one sentence.

Small businesses need you to burn your fingertips. They need you to know the business inside and out. They are not there to simply view as a fashionable item. Yet people do just that, then are bewildered at how they lose their ass in a financial tailspin. When I've sold businesses, there are a certain group of people who survive and thrive. They are the people who were willing to put in the sweat equity to learn the business, inside-and-out. They were willing to go work for someone else before purchasing the business, before setting out on their own. When someone brings you the check, signs on the dotted line, there is an obligation that I personally feel toward trying to help them. With The Cider Barrel, I was on-call for several months, went well-beyond the norm, simply to ensure that the new owner was in a good place. But I cannot be a miracle worker when the new business owner decides to change over the brand. Once it becomes their business, once they change things entirely, it is really their baby to screw up. And then, you look back, shake your head, and move on. Like any relationship, you can only be emotionally present for those who want to engage. Anything else is merely spitting in the wind.

NETWORKING EVEN IF YOU HAVE NOTHING TO SELL

There are several ways to go about networking, whether it is with chamber of commerce, connection leagues or civic groups. But the start of it all is to have the ability to engage. You cannot hang back in these situations and win. People rarely come to you as much as you will have to come to them. One of the best lessons that I ever received was from an old man, who was not really networking, but understood the process. Mike was in his 80s and would stand at the entrance of the local rotary club that I belonged to. And every person who entered, he would shake their hand and say, "Welcome to Rotary." I thought that was interesting, so I started joining him. That 2-3 second interaction broke the ice with everyone who came into the room. He told me that what would occur later was that he would have those same folks (i.e. all of them in that rotary group), approach him to chat. Because he had welcomed them, so they felt comfortable with him. His stance was "I lost my wife three years ago, so it helps to have people who want to say 'hello' and talk to me later on." I don't disagree with this statement at all. And if Mike is willing to do this, you should think about doing this as well. Especially since, minus losing a life partner, you have the ability to engage people on a different level from their entry point into the event.

Talking to everybody means understanding that you shouldn't be selling them on an up-pitch of your product. You should want to engage, understand, know who they are. Everyone else in the room will end up focusing on the short sale, the thing that really won't sell as much as they hope it will. You instead should focus on the long game. Being remembered and remembering them. There is a touch-point system to all of this. Four or five times you've met someone, you've engaged, you've been thoughtful without selling, you will have earned name recognition. Whether they buy from you or not, they will know who you are and will convey that to others who likely will buy from you. Remember, you aren't just selling to them, you're selling to the people who they come in contact with who can be connected to you. That's the way sales actually works.

Often, people think of connections and networking as direct sales relationships. They pitch their product, the person gets excited and buys. That does less and results in less impact than you think. That is the confusion between a buyer and an impulse sale. A buyer is someone who is engaged in the long term. They want to buy because they truly need the product, they understand the person selling the product, or they can direct the sale of the product to someone else that they care about. An impulse sale is just that. Impulse. A person who may or may not purchase at all in the future. Because they wanted it once. They may never need it again. You have to separate that interaction between those who will become a long-term buyer and someone who is an impulse sale. While both are important, the long game of the long-term buyer attaching themselves to you, to the relationship that you have with them, is far more important than the impulse sale.

A great power that you have in all of this is to remember names. Everyone loves to have their name said back to them. Every single one. Because it allows them to feel as if they have presence, as if they are important. Especially when the person looking at them is repeating it back to them. Repeat the name to them three times when you meet them. Eyeball their nametag or when you get their card. Do whatever it takes to remember their name. When you see them the second or third time, repeating their name will instill it in your brain. I've had that power used on me by others. It makes me feel as if I matter in their lives. I've also had people go "Oh, I don't remember names, what was your's again?" and it's been a big turn-off. Even if you meet 1,000 people a day, remember as many names as possible. It will make the bigger difference that you remember their name, because then they will work at remembering yours.

One key that I've always found is that you do not wear a nametag yourself. I realize that this disrupts the apple cart a little because you are looking for indicators of who the person in front of you is, so that you can learn their name. But people are often "business card collectors" who aren't really engaging with you enough to learn your name. They collect the business card, stuff it in their pocket, then move to the next person. That isn't a touch point. That's a person who really isn't investing in who you are. So, not wearing a name tag, you end up having them shake your hand, ask your name, which breaks the ice a bit. And by learning their name, talking them up the next time that you see them, better things occur. Suddenly, it's not only a challenge for them to remember your name, it's almost something necessary, after all, you took the time to remember theirs'.

This is powerful stuff. As it provides you with a bit of allure. People will want to know the guy who not only works the room, but doesn't have or require a name tag. In this tech age, people have gotten too comfortable with their comfort zones. They don't attempt to meet new people to engage, only to sell. This causes them to have an issue of diluting their actual networking ability. Great, you connect with someone on a social media platform such as LinkedIn or you collect their business card, but are you really developing a relationship with them? Are you really engaging and understanding that there are many things that you could be talking about beyond the norm? Those who resist networking entirely, or the machinations of it, aren't doing themselves any favors. I knew a massage therapist who was totally off of social media entirely, didn't like doing chamber networking even when there was the potential for a free ribbon cutting at her business by the chamber, and she ended up wondering why her clients tended to be less and less as time goes on. Because when you don't engage, people don't engage back. It is a symbiotic relationship. Either you give or you will not get.

Another understanding of any networking group is that everyone else is likely there to sell, not there to actually buy. Most are trying to get the impulse sale or get that quick relationship that earns them enough business to cash a commission check. Fewer are there to actually generate a larger relationship, where they understand and engage in the development of a process which is deeper and more meaningful. When you chat these folks up, look at what they are selling. See what it is that they aren't doing with their product or service. This is a great lesson for you, as you attempt to develop a relationship with them. Chances are, they won't give back as much as they get from you, but that's okay, you will separate yourself from them by giving more.

The way you win at networking is to give. Be a connector between two folks. You may not see the long game at first, but it exists. The more that you help, the more that you end up getting. People will like you because you helped them and they will remember you. Especially when you remember their name, help them, then suddenly, they will want to really remember yours and pay it forward. This is a device of networking that not enough people use. Try to see ways to connect two people who will help each other. I knew an ultimate connector who would approach two people selling two different things at networking meetings, let's say sales person No. 1 had a service and the sales person No. 2 had a product. He would go up and bring the idea of how that service could be used by sales person No. 2, and how the product could be used by sales person No. 1. You are essentially crafting a plan for quid pro quo which is Latin meaning "this for that." When you create ideas of how people can work together, suddenly, the two sales people, who otherwise would not have come up to that conclusion on their own to work together, will see it. Both sales people would have only seen their service or product being sold to the other sales person, not that both could be purchased and used effectively.

This is about providing ideas. That ultimate connector was also a business development person. By doing that for the other two sales people, he placed them in his debt without saying anything about it. The other two sales folks would usually go around the rest of the networking group, mention what was done for them by the ultimate connector, who would end up getting more business without even introducing himself. Because that's how networking ultimately works. The idea that Zoom or online meetings or social media is going to build up the connection as fast or as well as in-person connectors is silly. Because people can always erase or junk an email request. It's harder when someone is looking you dead in the face, wanting to talk and build that connection personally.

All of this is to say that you need to sell by being a good person. Even a great person. Smiling, with the ability to engage. You have to do it on their level as well. Don't jump their shit if they happen to say things in a bit of a coarse manner. I knew a banker who liked to exchange mind-fuck pickup lines with other men, things that could be said to women. Sure, is it sexist? Potentially. But was the banker merely having fun? Of course. And sometimes gallows humor works as a connector. The trouble was that one sales person who was new to the game decided to jump his shit. The new sales person tried to get the banker in trouble, shame him in front of the rest of the networking group, who knew the banker was overall a good guy, just saying some funny yet shady stuff. What occurred is what no one in a classroom or book usually will tell you. The new sales person was "iced" out at every other networking group. Few people would talk or engage with them. Mainly because no one likes a snitch. And second, because no one wants to be the next person that the new sales person was "offended" by and would otherwise be shamed later. Think about the image that you create for yourself. The networking folks had gotten to know the banker enough that they were willing to have a blind spot to his bullshit. They didn't know the new sales person enough to render that same judgement, so the new sales person lost out. Being right is not a bullet proof vest.

Too many sales people attend functions just to do a sales pitch. Because that's the way that they've been trained. They've been trained to perform the elevator sales pitch as if it's a jedi mind trick. That somehow, this will render the prospect unconscious to simply buy. This does not work. It hasn't worked for 50 years, yet sales trainers love to train this outdated, unproven model. Because it sounds correct. Much like single mothers who warp their young sons into believing that men should not be aggressive, etc. when it comes to dating. Those same young men learn quick that they will lose out to aggressive men, because 5000 years of D.N.A. in women showcase what attracts them to men. People aren't always correct in what they think compared to what they respond to. Whether you like this paragraph or not, the exception proves the rule. And women haven't stopped loving the bad boy.

When you are part of a civic group or any type of networking connection, it is imperative that you jump in to participate. Remember that old man, Mike, who greeted people at the door with "Welcome to Rotary." He did what he could to participate. If that's the measure in which he participates, he is still doing so. He isn't hanging back, sitting by himself, etc. Too often, folks that bitch about a lack of business out of a chamber lunch forum are the first people who get their meals, sit down around all of their colleagues from the office, and start eating. That first 30 minutes prior to a chamber lunch forum program starting is the actual gravy train period to build connections. You should be shaking hands, engaging with people, and approaching folks who are around you. If they have a fork and plate in front of their face, go up and shake their hand, disrupt their bullshit. You make that connection, build up your touch points, and force them to engage. Chances are, it will be something that they talk about with their colleagues around that eight chair round table during the rest of the meal. How you engaged with them, who is that guy, what does he do, etc.? Aggressive networking works because you are ensuring that no matter what, they have an opinion about you.

When you are at these chamber or networking functions, look for what they need as well. Can you run the check-in table for them? Do they need a booth guide or someone to help out collecting business cards for the raffle at the end of the program? All of these things are methods for you to build up your profile and connect with new folks. Don't just contribute, be aware of your surroundings. See what you can do to engage, network and remember the people that become a touch-point for you. Then, when you see them at another function, remember to engage but remind them of how you know them: "Lucy, it's been a minute since that last chamber forum. How have you been?" This automatically puts most networking folks back on their heels a bit, forcing them to realize how they know you. It provides a comfort factor as well, because they aren't simply meeting you for the first time, even if they forgot meeting you from the first time. It also forces them to remember or work at getting your name down, because you obviously remembered them. There is a bit of shame there. They don't want to be the person who is too myopic to remember you.

The last thing you want to do is go to a networking meeting and engage with the same person twenty straight times. These people can become vampires of your time. You only have about 30-45 minutes before the program starts, and these folks will want to engage with you, not because they want to network, but because you become a safe alternative to networking. After a bit, they aren't really networking, they are using you as a comfort blanket to say that they went out, they networked, and then they went home but didn't get any business. This is one of the major downfalls of effective networking, often, you end up providing too much comfort to people who aren't going to do anything but find ways to isolate you, because it benefits solely them. The best way to handle this is to rip the band aid off quick. Do a 2-3 minute chat session with them, and then excuse yourself because you want to grab a coffee or food. They will likely let you leave. You will then be able to engage with other folks networking, because the vampire will stay where they are. Vampires don't like to leave their corners, for fear of engaging with folks who they do not know. This is a way to move through that territory effectively.

You need to constantly have a 20 percent new engagement approach toward networking. That means finding 20 percent of the new folks in the event or group to chat up. Even if you have zero interest in them to buy anything or whatever, chat them up at least a few times. You need to own it and burn through it. Make sure that everyone is engaged with you because you are engaged with them. You will thin the herd as new folks come into the group, have questions, and then you can be the one who attempts to answer. Always go with the side-hug approach if it's members of the opposite sex. Always get a high-ball glass but ask the bartender for an Arnold Palmer with no straw. Your ability to be sober as well as appear as if you are drinking, will matter. You want to be the first person that people meet, but not the sloppy drunk that people avoid. I knew an insurance guy who was like the drunk cousin at a wedding reception. Always get way too loaded, couldn't figure out why people didn't buy from him. Because people are forming opinions of you left and right. If they see you as a sloppy drunk, they don't care what your low rates for their business are. They care about the image you are setting for yourself and others.

STARTUP 101

Starting any business means that you must be adaptive to the ideas and changes of the public. They are the ones buying whatever product that you are selling; whether that is a brick & mortar product or an internet distributed product or a consulting product. You either change, or you adapt or die. Adaptation is one of the more difficult things in business, specifically because once someone gets locked in with the germ of an idea, that's the idea that has stuck, guided them through the entire process, allowed them to fall in love with committing time, energy and finances toward creating a business around that product. And then, there is heartbreak, learning that the product's usage or need may be ahead of its audience, i.e. the need for the product now won't be what the need for the product will be years from now.

This type of situation can occur in several different forms. Imagine if the personal computer was created in the 1960s rather than the 1970s. It may have not achieved the investment level, or interest, nor would it have attracted Wall Street traders to buy into it. Mainframes may have continued to survive until the 2000s at that rate. Same with Amazon, if it had existed in 1988 rather than 1994. That seven year span may have had a negative effect, with a company that could have been killed by a lack of cash flow, while still retaining the killer idea that few would have adopted or wanted.

When you start a business, any business, you need to realize the quick rate in which the killer idea may be killed. Specifically, it comes down to whether you can survive long enough to catch on with your audience. The buying public isn't always aware of anything you do, no matter how much you want to spend on that idea. Things like this take time, as much as energy and finances, in order to potentially achieve success. Patience is one of the many things that business startups rarely have enough of, and end up capsizing because of. Finances are only a small portion of the overall issue with a business on whether it succeeds or fails.

The larger question is what type of business is this to you? Is it a royalty or an actual job? This matters. Too often, people work jobs like royalties and royalties as if those are jobs. The conundrum is whether you are understanding what business you are in, how much dedication it requires, and whether it is smart to merely "exist" rather than actually move forward, re-invest in the actual business, and build something up. Royalties should be considered more of a luxury, something that goes into a bank account for a rainy day, makes for a good tax write-off, and has the potential to be sold to someone else under an LLC agreement lease to purchase sale. The reason you keep a royalty around is to show that the majority of it, beyond cost of goods (COGs), are worth someone else purchasing. That's what a royalty is really all about: A passive income on a product sale, such as a candy route or a book sale, in which the COGs don't change, the amount of energy and effort is minimal, and the income is fairly consistent. Unfortunately, people like to cash in on royalties, using them in lieu of a job, so they don't have to do anything. Which is how people lose entire sums of money, once that royalty line ends, or the public's appetite for that product dies off or changes entirely.

A job on the other hand is just that. When you go into business for yourself, anything which requires a lot of effort is a job. That means YOU have to work it. That means YOU have to be the decision-maker, always on call, etc. Unlike a royalty, the job needs your face daily. It doesn't need you hanging out, relaxing, while others work. That's how businesses die off, because the owner never decided to spend enough time working the actual job. They instead wanted to have something that generated money, like an investment, believing that all it takes is money in order to survive. This is a great way to lose a lot of money as well as a business entirely. I'm not advocating being a control freak, but you have to dedicate a lot of time in order to make your business hum. Too often, the opposite is the case. Whether those owners want to admit it or not, they took a laissez-faire approach to the entire operation. They chose not to really know their employees, their product, or their distribution toward customers. They immediately thought that money would solve all things, while expecting never to lose any money on the business while also living off of the business. That's not how business works. If you want to never have to worry about a paycheck, work for a government agency or something to where you only earn a consistent amount of money each week and that's it. Working for yourself, in a job that you created, means you are required to be accountable to yourself.

The key to what you do as a business is Always Be Learning (ABL). When you learn, you know more, and the more you know about your industry, the better you are because of it. Specializing in only small parts of an industry's specialty doesn't help you if you sell everything. But if you specialize in only one product, you can specifically hone in on what makes it different, unique and worthwhile for customers to purchase. I always think of ABL whenever someone chats with me about the industry that they are in. I may not have business yet specifically in that industry or segment, but it's good to know more about it. I've learned about the ways toilets operate, the way that food is moved from place to place, and the amount of permitting requiring for a laundromat. I don't have money invested in a laundromat, but you never know, and it is good to learn more about it. When you shut off your ears, you shut off your mind, and not knowing something disallows you the ability to invest in opportunities or understand things further. I often see people close themselves off to risk, even listening to what is possible, simply for the avoidance of losing out on anything. When they do so, often they lose out on everything.

That's the rub when it comes to business. Few people wanted to back Jeff Bezos at Amazon back in the early 1990s. Mainly because it was an untested, risky move. Now, in the 2020s, everyone would love to go back in time, as if using that knowledge of the future would help them with the past. The thing is, people back then didn't see something that would emerge as the biggest force ever in all market segments, because they weren't adaptive or open to the ideas that were offered. Small ideas become big ideas later on. You just have to listen, learn and see what works.

There was a small movie theater that I tried to work with, using my ticket company as an offering. They refused to do so, specifically because they felt they could use an online ticket company to do the same thing. Then COVID-19 hit, they were bankrupted and the theater with no tenant had to go up for sale. They weren't willing to listen to what my ticket company could do; specifically market and bring them new customers who could have helped them book out enough shows to survive the pandemic. They may not have survived anyway, but they were unwilling to learn. When they forgot the ABL of business, they turned themselves off of potentially surviving and thriving.

Likewise, you may meet people who you can propose business dealings all day long, but the moment risk becomes a factor, they back off. There is no convincing someone of risking something if they are unwilling. Risk is part of the game. Yet several people want a no risk situation in order to thrive in. They want to find this world where there are no bills, there are no loses, and when you put a dollar into the machine, you will automatically get four dollars back. That sounds great, but risk is part of the overall game, and if you aren't willing to play it, you are going to be sitting on the sidelines, never striking out, but also never getting a base hit. Essentially, you are a non-combatant.

When you learn about anything, it is adaptive to whatever you are doing. It helps you create better systems, like a Rubik's Cube. Everything is a puzzle, especially when it comes to business systems. How things work, in order to create commerce, goes from both simple to complex. And it is up to you to understand how your business works, how systems can become more efficient, and how you can develop things better. When you don't try to learn or develop, when you aren't willing to let your biases go in order to know more about the systems in place, the setup and the organization, well, you lose everything altogether.

Some people refuse to learn new systems. Or they have the belief that they know it all before they begin. That person who walks into a restaurant, starts telling the cook, the waitstaff, and everyone else what is going on, when clearly, they barely know anything about how a restaurant is run. These things are what cost new business owners money, when they refuse to learn and they refuse to try to know more. Every system, including your own concept, will need to be consistently refined. Nothing is ever perfect. But if you let it get worse, if you don't try to fix it, the system will decay into something unmanageable.

You have to go eyes wide open into the industry or business that you are attempting to master. The hardest thing to do in life is to have money exchange hands. That's why they call it money. People don't willingly give it up, without you having to work for it. And you can attempt various methods in order to get money from them, including fraud, but even that takes a talent, that takes effort. Not that you should ever commit fraud, but hopefully you get the point, that nothing in this life is free, nor is money easy to obtain from anyone else.

An eyes wide open approach means that you see the books. You know the income. You know the losses. You know where the holes are and what is actually wrong with the system. Often, people see the gloss of a small business enterprise, fall in love with the concept, and then buy in, only to discover that the reality is much more dark, dank and horrifying. Because they closed their eyes right when they should have opened them. I see this a lot with folks who go into the business of coffee stands or food trucks. They like the flair of the customers standing in line, not the horrible conditions where they are standing during the entire shift, in a compact space over a hot iron stove or espresso machine. That's the issue with these enterprises, often, the person seeking to purchase one hasn't opened their eyes to the reality of what they are getting into.

Let's say that you are still gung-ho to move forward and purchase a coffee stand. Exactly who is your supplier of coffee beans? Of cups? Of lids? Of the espresso machine itself? Where are you going to put the stand? What is the lease like? How favorable are the conditions in order to succeed? Unless you know these things from the start, you are moving up a hill pushing a large boulder, with the inability to control your costs, which will quickly drain your capital. You have to know your product inside and out. That means everything from suppliers to distribution. That means when you choose to invest in a point of sale system (POS) are you getting a good POS system, or a piece of shit? It depends, mainly based on how much of your product, or conditions surrounding selling that product, are researched and developed before you initiate your plan. Belief is great, but knowledge is much better, especially when it's about turning a buck.

Not that this takes 50 years to learn how to do. Don't get me wrong. You could learn how to do some systems in a day or week. But it means you have to make the attempt to devour the knowledge of the entire system. From where you get the wholesale supply from, where it is made into the product that you can selling, and how you are going to distribute that product out to customers. I don't see a lot of folks succeed when they do not learn their product, or know what to do in order to curb expenses. Small business is not about making money as much as cutting costs to sell a product with the hope of making money; that might be lease payment renegotiations, employee hours cut in order to curb your labor expense ratio, or finding a supplier who can allow you to purchase in a great bulk for a reduction in overall product expense. These things matter, and if you aren't researching, and constantly developing ways to enhance the profit margin, while at the same time not losing quality of the product, then you aren't really in business. You are merely draining your capital, waiting for a foreclosure sign once your operation finally succumbs to the notion that the business model wasn't working from the start.

The inability for people to learn about their product, know what they are selling, is actually pretty common in small business. There are always people who go into something believing that "everything runs itself" and then they end up failing because of it. Let's say you want to go into a burger stand. That sounds easy enough. You just buy meat, buns, soda, etc. But when you suddenly figure out that you don't know about the equipment enough, especially refrigeration, and something fails, well, that didn't seem as easy as it looked, now did it? Just because something looks easy doesn't mean it's not very complicated in how it is produced and distributed. There are always a lot of variables, which is why some places fail. Plus, a lot of restaurants fail because people eat their own crappy cooking at home and don't realize that no one else likes to buy that same crappy cooking when they have a choice otherwise.

You have to know your industry. Thoroughly. Maybe there are too many burger stands in one area. Maybe there isn't enough volume of customer support to sustain it either. There's also the case of a person being utterly resistant to the idea of not doing a business in an area that clearly isn't ready for that business. Remember earlier when I mentioned owning a family fun center? After a short while, I was approached by a gentlemen about franchising a family fun center because mine was successful in a large county of 300,000+ people. He wanted to start a family fun center himself, in a town of 10,000 people with a county of less than 40,000. Basic math would tell you that he might have a more difficult time getting enough support. And yet, he kept finding himself resistant to the idea that it might not work. I don't know what happened to him, but I am willing to guess that he perhaps came to his senses, either that or he didn't and just went bankrupt because I never heard from him again.

This type of resistance to basic math, area demographics and customer interest is what people get stuck in their head, rather than actually try to know the industry that they want to go into. Specifically because they hate their current employment situation, they merely see it as a different distraction, without seeing the complications that come up along with it. A lot of roadblocks, including permitting, fees, etc. are just waiting to drain your capital. The taxes will come later. And there are always more taxes awaiting you. But that's just the start. You either can research, learn and know your industry prior to spending money, or you can do so after you've already committed yourself. The former will not cost you nearly as much as the latter will. Your choice.

My methodology in any business startup is to work for a competitor. That's right, they are your company's incubator. These are great ways to work for a week, for a month, writing everything down that they do. You want to know where their suppliers are? They will have you unloading the truck, meeting the supplier, getting business cards and contact information. Get hired by your competitor, and you learn all of their systems, what products they use and don't use, what methods work and don't work. And best yet, you quickly discover that you likely don't want to work in that industry, or have a business in that industry, within that period of time. It is a great way to know what the industry is like, eyes wide open, and whether you feel you could accurately fit into it.

I thought about owning a donut shop at one point. So I went 40 miles north and got hired by a donut shop, which had me do overnight production in their warehouse. What I learned was that making donuts is hard, the margins are very thin, the equipment breaks down a lot but is expensive, and it takes a lot of area to produce a lot of donuts effectively. After a few days, I quit the job (I don't even think I got a check for it) and decided not to go into the donut industry. I knew from the vantage point of working in that donut production line, how many hours of labor it would take, the equipment that it would cost and the suppliers, as well as the low margins. All of these factored not only into my decision on not doing the donut shop, but also ensuring that when I looked at other business models, I knew what it would take to run them alone, thus reducing labor hours, and foster a business model that would work in an industry that I wanted to be in.

Some competitors also do not know what they are doing. Even if they are somewhat functional. So these are great ways to create your own system of product creation and customer distribution, knowing how quickly the competition may fail against your startup business if you go to market. It allows you to effectively job shadow as the manager over-explains things to you. One thing that I've learned is that the employees talk. The managers are willing to let you know everything. No one hides any company secrets, mainly because most people are so academically lazy as to not take that information and go elsewhere with it. Company intellectual property, especially at the small business level, is so much about duplication that it doesn't matter. Take it, because they will simply try to copy your system later on anyway. Its only whether that system can be duplicated without any investment level on behalf of the competitor, to whether it actually sticks anyway.

Guaranteed your competitor has system flaws. They likely haven't adapted or changed their system since the 1980s when they were a startup themselves. Or they've only grafted on a pos system, rather than fully learning how to make theirs adaptive. This is your opportunity to create a better system in the process. You can also create your own relationship with vendors and suppliers, because you may end up being, quickly, the point of contact. What strikes me as interesting is that the manager of the competitor often will not seek out to be the point of contact for these suppliers and vendors, instead putting the newest person hired as the point designate. This creates an advantage to you, learning pricing and volume, of each item that your competitor sells.

You have to ask yourself why you want to be in this business. Specifically this business, what is it that matters to you? Why now? What about this business speaks to you enough to invest time, effort and capital into it? You are the only one that can truly answer that. You have to know right off why you're doing this, and once you dive in, head first, how you can rise back to the top, gasp for some air, and then keep swimming. Small business means understanding that you have to be prepared for what you are doing. You won't avoid challenges; there are always challenges in every business model or situations beyond your control, but you will be able to survive, based on the time that you put forth, preparing your business model to succeed.

Conversely, you have to ask yourself if you are too passionate for the business that you are going into. If you cannot separate yourself a bit, and be dispassionate enough to understand the numbers, you will fail. Even if you love this business, you will find that you can get blind spots quickly by not recognizing issues as their arise. You have to be able to see the warts of the business model, in order to change them for the better. It all comes down to whether you can be intrigued enough to help generate an income by perfecting a system, carefully researched and designed, with enough dispassion to know how to change things up if they aren't working.

Too often, entrepreneurs seek to quit their day job. They simply seek a start-up as another position in which to occupy their time, getting them away from the original job which they hated. They put all of their eggs into one basket, they work that startup as well as live off of its proceeds, and they end up going broke in the majority of the cases. Why? Because a startup at 1-3 years is not ready to sustain a livelihood. It requires that money to be re-invested in, and doesn't have the revenue to showcase actual financial support. A startup may generate a few dollars, even enough to break even, but every dollar is crucial toward putting back into the company, in order to make it thrive.

This is a telling sign of an entrepreneur who is more eager to leave a bad job position with another company than an entrepreneur developing a startup company that will be a powerhouse later on. Startups are young children. They need to grow. They need to crawl, then learn how to walk. Every dollar, even if there is a sudden need for the product, is absolutely crucial in the startup's development in order to build further. If the whole goal is simply to leave a crappy job, then you aren't going to win by starting your own company. You have to moonlight first. You have to do it off to the side, build up the business infrastructure in order to ensure that it will generate not only enough money for yourself to live off of, but also for the company's prospects not to be diminished once it supports you as its first employee. That means if you have a karate school idea, you need to train folks after your regular job, build up a clientele, then decide when it is time to quit.

The process of the young startup is to build out your entire company from scratch, using the most finite resource you have available: time. Money can only solve so many things. Time is what helps your startup grow, and if you just throw money at it, you often miss the mark.

Elizabeth Holmes with Theranos allegedly committed out-right fraud because she had the money, but not the time, to develop her product. Her start-up grew so fast that investors clamored for innovation to be solved immediately, rather than the start-up being afforded the time that it required for development. Holmes drained capital, lied to investors to keep them happy, and rolled out bad product which didn't function in order to meet money deadlines. That's what happens when an entrepreneur services the money end, not the innovation end, of the product. They fail themselves and their customers entirely.

A lot of people want to start businesses. They want to hit it rich. What they don't want to do is work at it. They don't want to spend the time and energy ensuring that their business thrives. Instead, they want to focus on how to spend the money generated by the startup on fancy homes or cars or a lavish lifestyle. Essentially, they want to win the lottery based on their idea without the implementation of a lot of hard work or risk. When I mentioned the lottery, your eyes likely rolled as a result. Because you understand how statistically, it is difficult to win the lottery. A lot of people will buy a ticket with an attempt to win each week, and it still doesn't make the odds at all great that you are going to win. Startups that survive, thrive and generate millions or billions in capital are no different.

If you want to work at a startup, you have to actually work at it for the hours required. If you want to make excuses, you don't need to waste your money doing a startup. This also entails using your spouse and children as human excuse shields for why you cannot work at your startup. Family takes dedication of time, energy and funds. If you don't want those things, don't have a family or keep one. That's your choice. However, you cannot expect kids to wait on you to decide when you have time for them. The same is true for a startup. If you create something, then let it languish, then complain about the fact that it did not yield, negating your involvement in whether or not you spent the time ensuring its development and success, well, that's on you.

Bank loans are not based solely on your startup idea. In fact, they are mostly leveraged off of your equity in a house or property. The bank wants an asset. Your startup idea is not one of them. However, they then position themselves as if your presentation on your startup matters to them. The brochures, the business plans, etc. If you have zero assets, your business plan won't matter even if you have a great P&L to show them. It's a game that the financial institutions play, to suggest that your business plan matters, but really, all it matters to is you.

Financial institutions want to see that you actually care, and are going to stick with the business plan, because it relates back to the asset. If you have a mortgaged asset against your business, then stop working your business, then the asset goes to the bank. And a bank doesn't really want the asset, they want the interest accumulated off of the loan leveraged against the asset, and so they end up selling the asset at auction for cheap to get it off of their books as soon as possible. Which is why they care about your startup business plan. Seems a bit of circular logic, but it pencils out if you think about it.

Being handed something is no guarantee that you will do something with it. Family legacy businesses (FLB) showcase that. After the first two generations, a FLB is usually ready to be sold. Doesn't matter the money accumulated due to the businesses either. It's about whether the passion is there to actually keep adapting the business, handed down from the dreams of a grandparent or great grandparent, to a new generation who may not be interested in sustaining and growing that business. FLBs usually have several children also fighting over the proceeds of inheritance, which complicates things overall.

Don't take this as an affront to FLBs either. It is difficult for a new generation to adapt the business and modernize it, because of the issue of past generations being present. The idea of too many cooks in the kitchen exists in FLBs. Even after retirement, the parent or grandparent is consistently questioning the moves to modernization that the new inherited and committed son/daughter makes in terms of business decisions. Their time passed, but they still want control while allowing someone else to do all of the work. Some of it is ego, some of it is worry that the business will be lost via poor decisions. And the child, now running the business, encounters the issue of not wanting to offend their parent or grandparent with any attempt for modernization. This leaves the FLB vulnerable to more agile competitors, along with changes in customer demand and interest.

Family in general can cause the improvement or destruction of a business based on how well they work together. If the parents and kids are fighting, or the siblings are fighting each other, the business ends up failing. So too does the business fail based on who the family members marry. A lot of business destruction is not merely based on spousal divorce, but how the spouses, who may not have any skin in the game originally starting the business, view the rest of the family members in the business. They may see the business as something that they can run without the other family members being involved. In reality, it is not who is right that matters when it comes to business decisions, but who has the power and who is listened to.

Economic storms come and go. It is whether or not the personal storms of relationships and life have a double-effect on the economic storm pending. There is always a storm brewing at some level. Mainly because life does not sit still. A startup has to be able to weather these storms, similar to a FLB. Taxation also comes into play when one family member dies, and the others are forced to cover any tax bills on land or business in lump sums or strung-out payouts. Folks that don't have the stomach for these storms needs to check themselves, and ask whether or not they are truly willing to face the reality of these issues overall. In most cases, they would be best suited to not attempt a startup, and in the case of a FLB, allow it to be managed by someone more suited for the opportunity and the risk.

Families can cause irreparable harm to businesses, even if they are not a part of the management team or a stakeholder. It depends on whether the family is supportive or destructive to the entrepreneur. Negative comments, the ability to influence others in the community not to purchase or presenting a bad image can be some of the ways that family cannot be supportive. This is no different than the circle of friends that an entrepreneur keeps. Are these friends successful? Are they innovative? Are they willing to listen and engage in your ideas? Or are they naysayers who are always presenting a negative attitude? Negative mentalities do not help situations, nor do they foster a lot of positive energy for the entrepreneur. Usually they are an energy drain, known as an energy vampire, and create an opportunity cost for the entrepreneur, as they tend to inject a negative mindset into the entrepreneur overall.

It is these types of risks as well as negative mindsets, that push entrepreneurs toward franchise opportunities. These are cookie-cutter methods of establishing a business, gaining a small percentage, on what is based on a "sound business model." Franchises are anything but, as they have flourished throughout the United States and world. Mainly because they don't innovate, they are usually a fad for a small 1-2 decade period, and they have territories for the franchise owners, which are often violated as expansion grows larger. Franchisees put up their equity, namely their house, and have to retain a minimum liquidity to operate a location. Franchisees also have to pay a 4-percent to 5-percent of gross profits back to the franchiser, along with every other cost, standard, etc. that may be different from state to state.

Franchises also close as frequently as they open, leaving the operators in a financial hole, while another franchisee opens up 10 blocks down the way. Franchises tend to look like they are a low-risk, but they are earmarked for expensive real estate such as malls and other places where the commercial rent is much higher. Also, franchises tend to find poor commercial property landlords, who don't take care of their buildings, and get locked into terrible leases, similar to anyone who creates a startup.

When people envision entrepreneurship, they think of instant success. What they will find, starting out for even the most successful companies, is a lot of past due and final notice statements in their future. Because making money takes time. It is not for the faint of heart. And you have to believe in something, especially believe in yourself, and play the long game. There is no sure-fire success model more important than playing that long game of keeping with sound business principles, avoiding negative naysayers and working hard to generate a profit. You will have to fight tooth and nail, and once you are successful at the venture, someone will suggest that you were too cutthroat or you did it the wrong way. Success looks easy to those who do not have any blood, sweat or tears to show for earning it.

You can create rivalries with competing businesses and waste your time worrying about what they do. Or you can ignore them, doing your own thing. My candy vending company once had a person who came into every place where I had a machine, attempting to undercut my percentage deal with the owner at a laundromat or car dealership waiting room. I gave 17-percent gross back, he offered up to 25-percent gross. They would be a fool not to take it, right? Nope. They held on because despite earning more money, I was someone that they had known, who they had dealt with, and I wasn't bothering them over a small percentage change when that's not their primary issue.

I could have made a stink out of it with the rival, could have done the same thing to the businesses where his candy machines were vending out, but instead, it wasn't worth my time. The worst thing you can do is let someone rent space in your head, but also occupy your hours for creating business with silly nonsense. I figured that if the laundromat or the car dealership waiting room or whatever other business wanted to leave me, despite me providing good service for their customers – which is really what they wanted more than the percentage back of revenue – then I wasn't a good fit for them anyway.

You have to feel that you are bringing something valuable to the table for your customers/clients. You cannot immediately drop your earning percentage to match others, simply because a new rival walks through the door while making promises. I only had one of the 7 locations decide to change out my candy machines for my rival's. And I did so. And in a few months, after the machines weren't filled, one of the rival's machine cannisters held peanuts which set off a peanut allergy of a customer in the waiting room – I refrained from stocking nuts for that reason – the location that dropped me then asked if I would bring my candy vending machine back. And I did so, but only gave them 10 percent, not 17 percent, gross profit back. Why? Because I lost revenue on their decision despite having a good relationship with them, and I didn't deserve to lose out. So, I now kept 7 percent more as a way of showcasing my displeasure. When you go against the family, there does come a cost.

Conversely, falling in love with your business, or your business model, is a recipe for disaster. You do have to change with the times. You do have to consider whether your best course of action is the best one for revenue generation. And that means understanding that sometimes, things will not work. Everything is a risk-hedge-bet situation. Constantly take in data, measure it and see what it yields. But at no time should you ever fall in love with the business itself. That creates blind spots. Because once you fall in love, it is harder to fall out of love, even when someone comes forward and offers you a big check to sell it, which should always be a consideration on the table.

You've taken the time to learn the craft, which is why you fell in love with it. You know all of the distributors, you get into a routine, and suddenly you see someone who hasn't done the work offering you a check to provide them with all of your years of blood, sweat and tears, essentially paying you to go away. The thing is, you don't have to take the offer, but you should consider it. You should always be separated enough from the business to be able to see that someone else might want to purchase it. And you should add 200-percent to whatever offer they choose to make. If they give it to you, and it meets that inflated asking price, you should take it. You can always restart, if you want to, which is why people don't sell when they likely should.

Often, people are frightened of starting over. That means a new concept, or new location, as well as risk. Because the old location did a certain amount, there is no certainty that the new location will do even close to that. The fear comes from not understanding that the issues with the old location came with inexperience. It came with not having a customer base that believed in you, developed over a 20-30 year period, and the fear that the audience won't come to your new location as they did the last. It is a baseless fear, but one that stops old businesses from taking the big check, then starting small with the next enterprise.

COFFEE MEETING ROULETTE

I would encourage any entrepreneur to do several coffee meetings. Chat with people in the community. Discuss everything in the know. Chances are, you will learn more about the market than if you open up your business with a shiny shingle hanging off of the corner of the building. Coffee meetings should consist of 30-45 minutes max. I would schedule several within 1-2 days, with different folks within the community. Learn more about the area, even if you have lived there for years. There are always little sub-groups emerging, as well as different components. You do not have to talk too much business, but let them know that you are considering opening up a small business in the community. Get their reaction.

If there is a fear that they will "steal" your idea and run with it themselves, then, welcome them to that opportunity. They will likely fail. And become your research and development department. They will not have the passion for the business that you will have. Nor will they have all of the insight that you are gathering. Remember that you are going to get your fingertips burnt. With your idea, they will not. They won't have the same drive as you will. And unless your business is an invention, they aren't developing anything new.

Jeff Bezos traveled to several bookstores around the country to learn what drove him nuts about bookstores. Availability for the actual book in question was one of them. But he didn't create a bookstore. He developed tech software which emulated a bookstore, then it eventually became an everything store. People can debate how people gain their fortunes, however, if Bezos hadn't been willing to travel those bookstores, sacrifice his time, energy and own salary at his New York hedge fund for an unrealized tech idea in Seattle, none of it would have been made possible. People enjoy belittling others' accomplishments, their drive, in order to feel better about themselves. Those "put-upon" folks who cannot see that everyone born isn't going to play in the All-Star Game, nor should they. Equality isn't the same as equity.

Coffee meetings are cheap and fun. You can also schedule several around each other, so that as someone is leaving, another person is entering to sit down. Schedule them at 15 minutes after the half hour - either at 2:15p or 2:45p. Then schedule the next for an hour later. What this does is psychologically get into the heads of the invited guest that this will be a brief coffee meeting, then you can casually pick their brain on everything. Have a point to the conversation, but make it about them. Mention that you respect their viewpoint, then ask them a few questions which lead you to better understanding the marketplace. This is how you learn about things such as distribution, permitting or taxation. All of the things that everyone avoids knowing about because it is boring, but will affect you in the long run.

I was once on a coffee meeting with a woman who shared my birthday, two years apart. She was much more open than I was, initially, because despite the idea that we might have the same astrological signs or grew up in the same era, we are different people. Sometimes, you meet mirror-opposites in people despite thinking there are similarities. This matters when you are considering how people are going to engage you. People have to meet the other person where they are at. And if you simply qualify or disqualify people's input without meeting them, you are doing yourself a disservice. Everyone has something that you can learn from.

One of the best opportunities to learn is when people are sitting around, with their guard down. If you want to become an entrepreneur, you should meet up with people who are also in the small business trade. They tend to be a lot more lax with their conversation, providing you more insight if you are willing to listen. I've always found people past their fortieth year of age to be much more interesting for this same reason. You cannot tell them who they are. They understand and have either resigned or embraced their flaws. Unless they are a trainwreck, they have dealt with enough in their life to be straight-forward in what they have as insecurities, or what they are sure of. When you meet with them casually, they also know that you are no threat to them, as they have accumulated enough knowledge of what their small business is, that even if you started today in the same industry, they would still always know more.

While it is not the same industry, I have found sitting casually with a cigar shop owner to be enlightening to the cider bar that I owned. He sold tobacco, I sold hard cider. But they were literally the same business: All retail-based. He sold wide selection as did I. But I also learned several things from our conversations. When new customers would walk in, unsure what they wanted, he would walk them through the selection, but talk them out of buying too much on the first shot. His premise was that he wanted them to use and enjoy the product, without attempting to be too consumed by the product's expiration. If they bought too much product, they would be less likely to enjoy each cigar, instead focused on smoking all of them before the cigars turned dry and went bad. There is a good lesson there: Try to build a customer for the long-term, not just the short-term.

In this same cigar shop, I met with a biker who also managed a towing company. He mentioned that he took extra classes on how to deal with electric vehicles, such as Tesla and Rivian. Most of the other tow companies had no inclination or interest in taking the 8-hour class on how to properly tow an electric vehicle. Thus, when they did so, there were often scratches or other damage issues because an electric vehicle being towed is unlike that of a gas-powered vehicle. From that 8 hour class, the biker had managed to have his tow truck operation become the automatic referral for several insurance companies, including AAA. This is when an 8-hour class transforms a business model and adds extra value overall to the scope of the core business.

What is remarkable about this cigar shop is that the knowledge sits there. It is accessed through casual relationships, where neither party is attempting to do harm on the other. They simply pass information. When I chose to ride a motorcycle, I asked the biker on various details of which used bike to purchase. When the biker's girlfriend was returning to school, he asked me various components of what transferring to different universities looked like. This is a casual exchange of information and it works. The old private business club models used to work like this. The guard is let down when you enter, people chat up a storm, and if you listen as well as digest, you learn a lot more than you can from anywhere else.

The goal is not to use people for information. But they can help you avoid pitfalls. This is much like a young woman's best friends are often her way to avoiding bad news men. My sister's best friends did more recon on any prospective boyfriend, knowing way too much about the guy, before he really stepped foot into her life. People do not build alone. They often require a tribal unit of others around them, in order to learn, develop and create the empire of their choosing. Arnold Schwarzenegger was an aspiring body builder in the 1970s, but also owned several commercial and residential properties because of his relationship with promoter Joe Weider, who pushed him toward real estate. While this wasn't the end-goal for Schwarzenegger, it serves as a lesson on how people learn from others. Schwarzenegger would not have had the continual resources to build his body building empire without the real estate revenue streams available to him. But Schwarzenegger started in 1968 with a bricklaying business, rolled the profits into a mail-order business for bodybuilding and fitness equipment, then purchased a $10,000 apartment building as a real estate investment. Now, he has several million in real estate investments, long after his film and political career has been over.

So, let's go back to Joe Weider. Imagine if he had not chatted with Schwarzenegger or mentioned the idea of real estate. Imagine if Arnold had not listened. Because Arnold wanted to be the best bodybuilder on the planet. Too many people focus on one area, not realizing that it is a multiple accumulation of everything around them. When you merely pinpoint precision focus on one area, you let everything else fall by the wayside. You see this with single parents, who often will suddenly want to get back into the dating scene. They will all consume themselves with one new person, almost eliminating or sacrificing the relationships with their children and friends. By doing this, they are not achieving a balance. They are obsessing with an addictive personality that doesn't allow them to see the rest of the gamut. By doing this, they actually cause harm to the overall life that they are trying to build.

With Arnold, he was a great bodybuilder, actor, entrepreneur, politician, etc. But notice, he did not pinpoint focus on one detail that eliminated all of the others. He also earned a distance-learning degree for a university because he felt it would serve him. And despite doing so, he understood the "joke" that he was a smart bodybuilder, which is a societal contradiction in terms. At no time did he not humble himself to the idea that he could learn or do more. This is a great lesson in how small business development works. You can either stand behind the counter of a retail shop that you own, doing the continual operation in the same way for 50 years, or you can continue to learn, develop and invest. Some of that investment comes through the education of others, some of it informal in nature, but just as valuable as any structured class might be.

When you decide that you are going to invest in something, anything, you should always take a deeper dive into what that means. That means watching your six, so to speak. I would chat with folks who have similar businesses. Find out what the holes are, where they are located, and whether you should prepare yourself for the idea that you will have to cross those chasms that are perceived as holes. A specific example of this is a local baker, who wanted to do donuts downtown. She bought all of the equipment, all of the resources, signed a lease, then discovered that the building was not prepped for Phase 3 power. That meant she would have to spend at least $25,000 to have the Phase 3 power upgrade to the building. Because she had already signed a lease, and the landlord wasn't going to do it themselves. And because she had already signed the lease, the landlord wasn't going to credit her with "tenant improvements" which mean reducing her rent because she was going to increase the building's value by $25,000 with the Phase 3 power installation.

Had the baker been on the lookout for community members who were landlords or tenants of other buildings, she would have known what to ask for in her lease. But she didn't. Ignorance is not an excuse toward success. Since I am laying this out for you as plain as day, take my advice, and seek out people to help you "know what you don't know." The problem is that this serves as a humbling experience. Several people might have met with the baker, free of charge, and told her things that she did not want to hear. Such as the Phase 3 power upgrade issue. It would have her confront her blind spot that the building may not have been suitable for her. That the landlord was a jerk that wouldn't negotiate with anyone. This is why wanna-preneurs often do not seek out other input: The information provided may not be what they want to hear.

I have a great friend whose late father and uncle owned several commercial and residential buildings. They taught my friend a lot about commercial real estate. But if you chat with him, you will learn more about public works than anywhere else. Public works is not something that is sexy enough to have an entire book written about it. Unless it is an academic book that will not fully engage with the reader. Much like the tax code. People know it exists, they have a vague understanding of it, but there is no real desire to understand it in detail unless it is their job. Except my friend is a wunderkind at knowing all about public works, from drainage to garbage to easement to covenant issues. This goes beyond anything his late father and uncle may have taught him. Despite this going beyond the scope of commercial real estate, it helps him fully understand the investment of taking on a new property or what costs may be associated with it. These buildings do not take care of themselves. They require a lot of work. And he at least has a fundamental understanding of what costs may arise and whether they are necessary to the function of the property's long-term health.

Conversely, you can also meet a lot of folks whose parents or grandparents determined their future enterprise, simply through the inheritance. The lineage either decides to inherit, but also learn the business in order to expand, or they are merely operators, facilitating the continual flow of the business until it collapses upon itself. The majority of family-owned inherited businesses collapse after the third or fourth generation takes control of the reins. Mainly because this wasn't their passion, but it does provide a stable income. They often go through the motions of operation, but do not adapt fully with the times, waiting for nimble competitors to remove market share. This occurs more often than not, specifically because the goal of a fourth generation family-owned business is to play it safe. Or there are far other interests driving that person, who never wanted to be in the family-business in the first place. A strange paradox if there ever was one.

Throughout your coffee meetings, you should be able to size up the market in many ways that are new to you. It may also help you understand various components of licensing, taxation and distribution. Especially what may be arriving on the horizon. These folks that you are meeting with could be considered subject matter experts. You will learn a lot from listening, engaging and asking great questions. This also means that you need to do further research, regardless of what you are being told, in order to ensure that you are gaining every bit of information possible. I would recommend doing all of this before even starting a business. Because that is when the meter has started to run; on the expiring product, the lease space, etc., Why not learn more about the prospective business prior to actually doing the business? Seems logical to me.

PEROT'S CADILLAC BIAS

People do not see the start of something big sometimes, even if they are a billionaire. H. Ross Perot was a Texas tech billionaire back in 1978. He had founded Electronic Data Systems (EDS) in 1962, after working at International Business Machines (IBM) as a salesman. Perot saw the inefficiency of the IBM systems when used by its customers, founded his company to help institute a technological LEAN management for insurers, banks and Medicare in the state of Texas. But for as able as H. Ross Perot was in spotting an advantage for EDS, he completely botched becoming the richest man in the world by passing on a $2 million dollar investment. And because of the silliest issues. His people didn't drive Cadillacs.

That is literally the quote which stopped H. Ross Perot from becoming the richest man in the history of the world by the 2000s.

"My people don't drive Cadillacs."

According to the 1999 book on Home Depot's origins, "Built From Scratch," dealmaker Ken Langone approached H. Ross Perot in 1978. Ken wanted Perot to invest $2 million dollars into the idea that would become Home Depot. For his investment, Perot would own 70% of the company. Yet, Perot's investment stalled once he was informed that the Home Depot start-up would lease Cadillacs to its executive staff. Perot refused to authorize the Cadillac leasing program to his executives. Perot wouldn't budge, adamant, and his $2 million dollar offer was shelved by Home Depot's founder, Bernie Marcus. After all, if Perot was that hardcore about what his people drove to work in, imagine what it would be like to work for him when the bigger decisions came around to be made.

By 1999, Perot would have earned $58 billion off of his $2 million Home Depot investment. By 2019, Perot would have had $200 billion more. Perot was a small, squeaky man who got aggressively into the 1992 U.S. Presidential race, upset the apple cart, and came away with 19 percent of the vote. He was concerned about mass deficits and the issues they had for larger generations. Except in 1978, he was concerned about Cadillacs. Enough that it cost him a large fortune. But don't feel too bad for Perot, he died in 2019 with $4 billion dollars. About $196 billion less than if he had only been accepting that some of his executives might drive nicer cars.

There are some lessons that Perot did learn, mainly from EDS. People were not simply numbers to him when it came to system functionality and deliverables. Sure, they couldn't drive Cadillacs, but the systems they bought needed to work right. Or at least, not be so cumbersome.

This comes back to customer service, or the lack thereof. If you haven't noticed since 2020, quality customer service has been lacking all of the way around. COVID-19 did a bang-up job on every organization reducing the idea of customer service, and for the most part, getting away with it.

There were places that needed to reduce customer service during the COVID-19 shutdowns and social distancing. And you can safely show enough examples of places that simply removed customer service entirely, because they didn't really think you had anywhere else to go either. Place your distribution hub example here. Warehouses that used to allow pickup for less, removed it entirely in favor of paid shipping. Other organizations simply removed their phone numbers from websites, stating that you could email them or deal with a BOT messenger to perhaps handle your concern. But quality customer service has been on life support for a while now since 2020 and it has only gotten worse. This leads to an advantage if you are willing to provide it as a small business. The difference is noticeable entirely.

You cannot deliver it until you are willing to give it. The idea of simply stating that you want to have quality customer service is a bit of a lie. It is something to where that rent is due every second of every day to every customer you meet. Including the horrible ones that make your life hell. Because quality customer service is not solely for those you like, but actually more for those you do not like. Your goal is to impress them enough that they are taken-aback by the entire situation. That they actually question themselves on how they have been acting toward you as a customer. It matters because when you put someone back on their heels with a better customer experience, they actually pause and re-evaluate themselves. It is one of the more perfect dynamics in the business-customer exchange. The issue is that you have to train this into your staff, who do not see the same dynamics, nor do they feel like they should always go above and beyond for the customers who are sour to them.

The experience should always exceed the price that the customer is paying. Think about how that works. Especially if your prices are higher than others. You are there to showcase why the price is higher. Because you deliver at a higher customer service rate of quality than your competitors. Some folks in the area will not get this. They are discount hunters. They are not folks who actually understand the amount of hospitality that you are attempting to deliver. With each action, you are either creating a fan or an enemy. It matters how you treat them, even when a customer clearly doesn't deserve it. Because of how others interact with the exchange between you and that customer. Everything is not a one-off either. Sometimes, you are showcasing to fellow customers that you have a higher level of customer service available in general.

Quality customer service starts by diagnosing the needs of the customer. That means that you ask questions. You engage with them. You make recommendations. If you are standing behind a barrier, such as a bar or retail counter, you really aren't engaging with someone as well as you could. You need to fully invest in an approach, in making it all about them. This is the time in which you do not focus on your phone, talk about yourself, etc. You instead need to fully invest in what their wants, needs and desires are. This brings presence to your conversation with them. They feel that they are engaging with someone who cares. A bartender friend of mine told me "pick your character and make sure it's entertaining." Because nothing else matters at all.

This is about making sure that every customer feels listened to and heard. This means that you are digesting what they are saying. It doesn't mean everything goes their way, but they can truly take in that you care, that you want to help them with their needs when it concerns your product, and making a better, informative decision. Being listened to is not about pandering either. You need to be able to help them evaluate what they are looking for, which may not be what they think they are looking for. Sometimes, customers don't know what they want. That's why they are seeking you as a conduit to help them make certain choices.

The key is not to sell them only on what they say they want. That's a fool's game because they don't really know what they want nor need. This is where you come in with quality customer service. When they have an issue, they need a result, they need a beneficial interaction which says that they will gain a better resolution to whatever the issue is. That means that if you merely sell them on more product, but don't solve their problem, you're actually making their problem more difficult. Because you weren't listening to them. You weren't helping them make a better decision, but only a decision which benefitted you. When you look at it that way, you can easily see that by merely directing them to a new product sale, rather than helping them figure out their issues and solve their problems through your products, you were being selfish, not helpful.

The reason that quality customer service matters is that you are looking toward the long-game of building up a buyer. This is that repeat buyer. The one who not only comes back to your business, but also directs others to your business. Because they felt like you wanted them there. They felt like you were encouraged to have them there and they want that feeling again, not just for themselves but for their friends. Quality customer service is about customer creation in the long-term vision. It only happens when you make them feel wanted, listened to and heard.

Don't simply sell units. You aren't there to move product. You are there to build customers. That means that while the product moves, there needs to be a connection behind it. Where you want the customer to belong. To return. To advocate for your business. Simply pushing units is a vapid response. It's doesn't yield out. Work harder to make your customers become more than just one time sales. They need to actually want to be there to buy.

Sometimes, customer service can be a bit too much. I learned this in 2003, while attending Eastern Washington University in Cheney, Washington. And the lesson originated from a squirrel that wanted a Fruit Loop.

Across the street from the EWU campus sat the Married Student Court, which had been erected back in the 1960s as an option for married students to live with families while attending the college. Each unit had a patio and sliding glass window, along with a little lawn. Enough that a family would not see the difference between it and a rental home, living cheaply enough to attend "the cheapest public four-year institution in the state of Washington." It was there, in 2003, that a squirrel desiring a Fruit Loop showed how far EWU would go to show its students customer service, in every wrong way possible.

The squirrel had managed to navigate through one of the Married Student Court lawns and onto the patio, where a child was eating her Fruit Loops. The squirrel grabbed one, nibbled on it, then was attacked by the child's mother, who swatted the squirrel with a broom. The squirrel escaped unharmed. And if that had been the end of the story, there would be no story. However, the mother's husband was a student worker for the EWU Facilities manager, and he got an earful from his wife. Enough that the husband told his boss, who told another boss, who mentioned it to the head of EWU Facilities. To this day, the vertical integration of a state university system at communicating this one issue - a squirrel robbing a child of a Fruit Loop - is an amazing feat that have made people with more important things jealous since that time.

Down from the hierarchy of EWU Facilities came the edict to do something about the squirrel population, which had been "deemed out of control." Because it is a slippery slope if one Fruit Loop is stolen, think of what will occur next if nothing is done. Squirrel world domination? EWU Facilities would have none of it. They prided themselves on customer service enough to call in an exterminator to reduce the squirrel population a bit. At least, make it manageable. And the exterminator, receiving the order, delivered quality customer service as well.

That April Monday morning of class, EWU students entered into the quad. I was among them. And before us was a squirrel reenactment of Gone With The Wind, minus Scarlett O'Hara. Over a thousand squirrel bodies laid dead throughout the campus. Minus wearing the uniforms of the North and South.

The exterminator had done his job in over-delivering quality customer service, enough that the squirrel population drew the attention of local news of nearby Spokane, 19 miles away from campus. Spokane's media rarely ever covered EWU, but now they did. Enough that the news went national, then international, within days. Before the days of social media, the story was a viral earworm that continued to last long enough that over two decades later, I ended up working with a colleague who also attended EWU at that time.

"Do you remember the dead squirrels?" She asked me.

"Yeah. Is that all you remember?" I asked back.

"No, but it still stands out the most when I talk to people I went to school with."

The exterminator was hounded for years after by environmentalists and nutjob animal rights people. EWU Facilities backed away from any responsibility, doing exactly what state university systems do in times of crisis. They ignored every media request and turtled as much as possible. All because a squirrel decided to steal a Fruit Loop. He along with his 1,000 other squirrel brothers and sisters, paid a heavy price.

Another adventure was back at my Seattle University days, in 2007, which you will hear about a lot during the course of this book. When you have adventures in college athletics, you tend to remember them. I was tasked with a huge printing and mailing project for the department. The office assistant told me to use the UPS Store on First Hill in Seattle, and to ask for "Agnes." I did as I was told. And from that moment, I feel in love with Agnes. Figuratively, not literally. Although, maybe literally. Agnes was a dynamo at getting my 1,405 pieces of individual brochures out with ease. She processed it all, didn't ask too many questions, and I was out the door, back to the office in less than 30 minutes. What a wonder.

In the next few months, I would rely on Agnes quite a bit. Sometimes, there were over 3,000 pieces of mail to go out for the annual campus Crab Feed and other fundraisers. Seattle University's mail system at the time had been circumvented by the LEAN management technology which said to contract out everything that the private Jesuit university could. So they did. Which meant that the on-campus mailing by an outsourced company was difficult and painful. And at one point, a campus administrator inquired why we weren't using the on-campus outsourced company rather than the UPS store across the street. I ignored this inquiry and continued to use Agnes. Until the day that she was no longer at the First Hill store. She had been promoted, moved to the University District next to the University of Washington campus about 12 miles away from First Hill. Which in Seattle terms can be a 30-to-45 minute drive due to traffic and the winding city roads of the greater Seattle area. I loaded up a campus van with the materials, went to the University District UPS store, and Agnes took care of everything. Done. Easy. Didn't think about it for more than 30 minutes at most. The drive was longer.

My athletic director, Bill, was not amused. He demanded to know why I wasn't using the on-campus outsourced print services. He had gotten an earful from that campus administrator. And Bill wanted to know why I required using a campus van to go to another university's UPS store. Why couldn't I use one closer? I told him that my reasoning was Agnes. Bill disregarded my comment, and said he would do the next mailings himself. Which he did. Using the on-campus outsourced company to mail it out. Took him nearly three hours and none of the mailings went to the right place. After that, he didn't challenge why we drove to the University District UPS store or why we swore by Agnes. Customer service is more than handling a product. It's making sure that the problem and pain point is fully taken care of in the first place.

COVID-19 KILLED JOB LOYALTY

People usually make attempts to work with others especially when the environment suits them. But when they end up finding no quarter for their ideas, or their ability to manage other people's difficult personalities, they leave. People can fire their bosses. I was chatting with a friend who was living in Texas about people leaving their jobs. He said that COVID-19 had proven that the social contract between working a long-term job had ended. That there was no need to consider a permanent job since both the job and the person may separate at any time. The shutdowns and certain states reopening, while other states doing mental gymnastics not to reopen, also proved that people were expendable depending on the political machinations of the state to which you resided in.

My friend also said that the way people quit was also changing. He had recently experienced a high level executive quitting via e-mail, providing a two-week notice while hitting the vacation button, instead of talking to the owner of the $200 million dollar company. The owner lamented that he felt his own relationship with the executive should have been enough to have the executive converse with the owner first. Do a face-to-face. Respect the owner so that he could show respect back to the executive.

I said to my friend: "Isn't that the actual problem? The owner isn't asking himself why they weren't really proactive enough to avoid this type of resignation in the first place. Instead, he's blaming the victim."

"Yeah, but my owner isn't going to listen to that."

A large reason that people start their own businesses is not to work harder. It's to get away from a job that they do not enjoy. They feel working for themselves will be easier. And honestly, they start working for themselves with the idea that they won't be working at all. That they will be paying someone else to do a function. Then, they end up going off of their short runway. They do not have enough speed to take off, nor do they have enough money to sustain their lifestyle when the paychecks aren't automatically coming in.

Whenever you decide to do an entrepreneurial endeavor, it is important to examine your runway. That's the amount of capital that you have under your control which can be liquid enough to survive until people start buying. It's a funny term, runway, because this endeavor that you are on is a gigantic airplane carrying all of your ideas. And if you run out of runway before you can take off, well, your plane is going to crash, much like your business. It is smart to realize how you can maximize your runway by expanding on how fluidity of capital works, such as delayed payments and cash flow overall, but you need to know this measurement overall. Otherwise you are certainly not going to make that flight take off before the end of the runway hits. And that's tragic for everyone on board, as well as everyone watching back at the terminal who were your potential customers hoping that your business would take off.

The runway isn't just about when your doors open. Consider the issue of permitting, which usually delays everything. Whether its health department, liquor control board or simply building permits, everything can delay your eventual opening. These are things that you are certain to plan for, yet they always emerge when you've already signed your lease and the clock is ticking until your next commercial monthly rent payment. The plane is starting to take off, but the runway has to be long enough for the plane to have somewhere to go. And sometimes, that runway may have to be over a year in advance of existence before revenue is actually generated at the endeavor.

That leads to another issue that occurs constantly: People quitting their origination job that they hate immediately when they start an entrepreneurial endeavor. This might not be possible. You're adding a weight as a thumb on the scale against success for your business. Specifically because now that business has to have a way to support you from the start, even when it is just starting to discover who its customers are. That may not be immediately possible. And it shortens the overall runway that you have, because that limits the amount of capital available. Now, instead of merely covering the bills of the business, it has to cover you as the main employee, whether it has other employees or not. The goal of your initial runway is to ensure that even if you have employees, the business can exist for a longer period of time without worrying about initially generating money. Because it won't from the start. Customers don't immediately come around and buy. It takes time to build an audience.

There were a lot of businesses that died in 2020 and 2021 because of COVID-19 which had not created a large enough runway for themselves. Specifically in the bar / service industry. Not only did they not have the resources to match overhead issues, they also did not pivot their business toward ways to make money. This goes beyond a PPP loan debate or some grant money that would have covered rent for two days of operation at a large bar. This is about that bar understanding that they would have to change their business model to fit the new era of revenue generation, instead focusing on the old way of operation which was no longer relevant. That's a component of the runway that no one ever talks about: Can you weather the weather? That is, can you survive when everything hits the fan. No one thought that COVID-19 shutdowns were going to happen, but they did, several times. If you owned a bar and refused to pivot along with the shutdowns, you weren't to make money. And that's when the runway starts to run out underneath the tires of your plane before it can lift-off and take flight.

The COVID-19 shutdowns revealed that when bars were forced to close for sit down dining, that most just shut themselves down and acted like that business model would return after some time. As 2020 extended from Spring into Summer into Fall, a lot of those bars / restaurants should have used the "to-go" options available and transformed into grocery stores for their booze and food. Too many of them instead fought against the delivery apps. Too many of them instead refused to install giant racks filled with bottles of booze, cans of beer, etc. They didn't see that this was an option to continue making sales. Instead, they waited for the rest of the world to rejoin their old business model, which was no longer relevant. At the end of 2021, most of those restaurants were basically waiting for non-existent federal aid and other bail-out protections to keep their tired business model going. Good luck with that runway as it disappears beneath you and your business crashes and burns.

Another factor is customers. Sure, everyone who is your friend will show up on the first day to celebrate your new business. But what about the twentieth day or the two-hundredth day? Getting people to buy in to what you are selling is difficult enough without making assumptions that you don't have to work for their business. It is a constantly, consistent hustle to push for new business. And if you decide to not prepare, once the doors are open, all it takes is a few days of emptiness in your establishment for you to realize that you didn't plan enough for it. This is the line of demarcation between a true entrepreneur and a wanna-preneur: Whether you are prepared to actually build up a customer base or not. It is a constant, big grind.

Preparing for your runway means that you need to also know about lease rental increases and repair issues that might come up. You need to be sure that when things occur, you are already prepared for them. You should have an emergency fund set aside to handle these types of losses. They will come and they will be frightening to your business. The same can be said for quarterly taxes. Everyone always thinks they have more money than they do until the federal and state government taxation machines move through. Then suddenly, they have less than none. Your runway gets shorter the more that you avoid looking ahead. It dissolves because you kept your eyes closed to the possibilities. The runway only grows the further that you see from beyond the edge of the plane's nose. When you look out as far as you can, prepare for it, and have capital set aside, you will be ready for lift-off as customers start walking through your doors, not simply the first time, but as repeat customers, over and over again.

One obvious goal is to do as little as you can thru government regulation. This sounds shady, but hear me out on what I am talking about. Do you need a business license in order to function? That costs money. And you have to report every dime quarterly to the state, so they can tax you more. If all you are doing is a small amount of business, I would avoid it. I do not think you should open a large restaurant, bar or cigar lounge without a business license and the proper regulation. Unless you want the FBI, ATF, gambling commission and state liquor board knocking on your door. But if you are not generating a sizable profit flipping China plates, and if you can take cash, then why report it? Do you really need a "resellers" permit for that? Why join the tournament at the low-end of the spectrum when you aren't really generating anything of consequence?

The difficulty is knowing when to go public and join the tournament as a fully-fledged business owner. Getting all of the licensing, taxes and potential impact fees out of the way from the start. The super far left tends to gloss over these machinations until I have them propose a business. After we walk thru every component, including taxations, fees, etc., they seem more comfortable to stay in their state office or nonprofit job, complaining about the greed of others. Those that can do, those that can't end up thinking everyone else is greedy. If you notice, the people who have the bright idea of giving everything away are the ones with nothing to lose who aren't really producing anything to begin with.

I had this issue with a co-op diner in downtown Olympia during the pandemic. Sitting right across the main avenue from my cider bar, the co-op would not allow vagrants or homeless to be trespassed, including during hours when they were not open. The vagrants would also sell drugs, walking across the street into my alcove to avoid "getting the co-op in trouble." My security cameras would catch them operating the drug deals. I tried talking to the co-op folks, but they refused to listen. They called me a "greedy capitalistic pig." Frustrated, I looked up the building's insurance through my insurance agent, then called the insurer, who was in Chicago. He had no idea that the co-op was willing to violate their agreement by allowing illegal drugs on the premises. He took care of it. Within a few days, the vagrants were gone. I found the co-op's pain point and used it to get a response. Sometimes, it's about knowing where to go and what to do that matters most.

WHAT IS YOUR EXPERTISE?

A lot of people see the marketplace and do not understand that there is always room for those who can create added value. Kelly was one of those people. She worked in mess halls for the U.S. Army for 29 years. She designed dishes for years. And when she exited the military as a retiree, she decided to make chicken wings as a business. Consider what she was doing. Chicken wings are damn near impossible to create as a functioning business model separator. How could it? Every business makes chicken wings. Same as everyone makes a burger. There are really no ways to merely function in delivering chicken wings which will have customers cross the street specifically for your wings.

Kelly didn't give up. Nor did she start her business in a routine fashion. She went old school. Kelly brought her chicken wings to business networking events. She allowed people to eat up, sample more, and built up an audience. Then she made attempts to do catering out of her kitchen, only to have the county's environmental health department shut her down. Seems she didn't pay for a $600 permit to have them checklist her kitchen as safe to serve. But Kelly didn't give up, she kept going, even during COVID-19. Enough that she financed part of her Ikonic Wings store with her military retirement money. She took a risk, including during the continual Governor Inslee shutdowns occurring in Washington state.

Kelly kept building out her store, going against the grain. She did not include seating in her store, only pick up, without a drive-thru window. Insane. Yet, the county's pandemic $100k grant was provided to Kelly, who used the money to finish out her store. And yet, her store has thrived and survived. Word of mouth about her wings has grown in the two years that she has been open. Kelly survived because she had one thing on her side; she was an expert at the craft of cooking chicken wings. Large wings. Enough that kids referred to them as "dinosaur wings." Imagine the reputation boost, the separator where there is supposed to be no separator, and yet, it occurred because Kelly had an expertise. She also eliminated overhead by ignoring the notion that she needed sit down service, focusing solely on hiring staff to cook wings and nothing else. Literally, Ikonic Wings serves wings. Not burgers or fish or anything else. Simply wings. And they are fantastic at it.

Are you willing to become an expert in your field? Are you willing to know way too much about this product, this industry, this business? That is what it takes this day to convince someone to buy your product continuously. Your obsession. You need to obsess. You need to be so self-absorbed with whatever it is that you are selling in your stores that you are an expert in your field. That means doing your research, understanding the nuances beyond a google search. You need to be in-depth with your industry. People are no longer satisfied with purchasing anything, they want, need and desire an expert to help them.

SMALL BUSINESS SCHOOL

I was in the Macy's department store recently. The men's suit section. Looking at various sport jackets and suits, unsure what to purchase. As the founder of the Men's Warehouse George Zimmer wrote in his 2021 book, "I Guarantee It," men hate to purchase anything at any time in public. They hate the process. The inability to simply grab and go. Men do not what to be there. And yet, no one has ever understood men outside of the Men's Warehouse, which used to have the ability to be sized up, and out the door as soon as humanly possible. At the Macy's, as I tried on a sport jacket, a woman working there walked by, eyes down, as fast as possible. This is not an indictment of her as much as the trend that has occurred with online culture: We are now order takers, not concierge service. No one who knows a lot is in one area of the store, serving as an expert to help you with anything.

Feel this from a customer point of view: If you are simply another place without anything of benefit, why would someone purchase from you? Why would they care? The staff at that Macy's, or any department store, are generally there to either ring up an order or keep you from walking off with the stuff. And you're treated as if you are a number, rather than someone of value that they want to have as a return customer. They have now become the physical version of analytics: They simply wait to have you return to buy because you see their sign, rather than the direct relationship that you might have with their store staff.

We have gotten away from expertise. We have deemed it too costly. The more that A.I. takes over on specific areas of employment, the more likely that the only difference will be the expertise of the employee toward the customer. As much as A.I. likes to be shopped around as the answer, it is often less of a solution. It gathers information, but it does not dole out variances in option. To A.I., there is only one answer, and never a suggestion based off of eye-balling the customer, which can help the customer more than up-sell them into a higher end product. This is where the human expert supersedes and will always supersede the A.I. counterpart.

But when we do not provide experts. When we do not hire or train employees to understand the nuances of the customers that they are serving, we lose out to automation and A.I. completely. Think of the bookstore where you have the one person who knows every type of book you may like, because they also read it. They didn't just suggest it based off of your purchase history. They read the text of the book and thought that you would like it as well. That still means something when a customer is provided with that response. People love to hear the opinions of others on a product, not merely to be sized-up for a sale, but to gather whether they will enjoy it as well.

There is a distinct reason for film criticism that has been lost since the death of Roger Ebert and Gene Siskel. They had a following because they didn't act like merely snobs toward films that others would have considered "popcorn fluff." They saw it as entertainment, understood that the public may watch a film as escape, and reviewed those films accordingly. Some of which would never ever be considered worthy of an Academy Award. But they still provided an expert opinion with a dissection of film history. Consider the gap left now, when the majority of the film reviewers appear to have no interest in film that was put on the silver screen prior to their own watching lifetime. There's something missing there, you can tell, which is why the majority of film critics have no traction, no national name, and cannot provide anyone with a credible viewpoint that helps an under-marketed film get traction.

This is where Macy's failed me. As other stores have as well. And it is a good lesson for anyone deciding to run a business. I was in the market for a suit. I was ready to purchase. Yet, without the expertise of anyone staffed at the store, I tried a few things on, considered them, then grabbed my phone, looking up similar items on Amazon which were sold for cheaper. When you offer your customers nothing but the difference in price, that's what they will go for. But when you offer customers a difference of localized expertise, the fact that you may have other alternative suggestions beyond what an Amazon search can get them, you'll always win out. People love to tell someone that they "know a guy" or "know a gal" who can help them directly with a product purchase. An expert in a room.

EMBRACE YOUR CRITICS

Small business owners have an issue with criticism. Mainly, we feel that all criticism is the same, equal in its value. Nothing could be further from the truth. It is one thing to be criticized by a fellow small business owner for your practices and efforts. That should sting, mainly because they know what you are going through, in every facet from permitting, to taxation to sales. However, when you get someone who is not a small business owner, who hasn't stuck their neck out at all, criticizing your own small business, delivering a sermon on how "things to be run" and how "you are greedy," well, that is a whole different ball of wax.

Social media is a cesspool of village idiots. The "put-upons" who believe that everything is hopeless, that they somehow got screwed over despite making terrible ill-advised choices, and that it is always someone else's fault. They only laud stories where rich people gift their money away. Because, in their mindset, everyone who earned more than them did so in an unfair manner. This cyclical methodology of "put-upon" madness should be shunned, yet is somehow embraced as fact.

None of these people accomplished anything with their lives. They did so knowing full well that making bad choices would lead down a bad road, yet they did so willingly. Yet, accountability is not something they would accept.

Let's break down one of the biggest: cigarettes and alcohol. These are both addictions, now labeled as health crisis such as a disease, because it allows more societal acceptability when something is attained not through choice, but by random virus. So be it. But these folks know as they do these features, prior to starting, that they are going to be spending a lot of money doing it. A pack of cigarettes costs $9.79 as of December 2024. Smoking 1-2 packs per day, you can see that this easily adds up to over $100 a month. Alcohol is no different. And I've sold alcohol prior, so I understand how some people just have to be cut-off by the establishment so that they will take an unwilling break in the action. But all of these methods have consequences, in terms of how much money you cost yourself, rather than save.

This is not to beat up on someone with an addiction. It's to show how fast someone can spend a lot of money that they obviously should rather not spend on a temporary item. The same is true for fast cars, large houses, etc. One of the old world models of wealth-building is to purchase a house. Invest and pay off the mortgage. However, what this does is cement you into one area, one community, and hopefully, you do not lose your job in the meantime. Otherwise, the house that you put 10 years of mortgage payments into may be going at a large discount. Meaning you got nothing really of value in the sale itself. I am not a firm believer in purchasing a house unless you plan to die in it. You need the ability to be mobile, move as much as possible, to ensure that you are able to maximize your profit potential when opportunities come knocking.

Yet, the critics of you, of your business mindset and business model, do not care about the amount of taxation, permitting and other issues that arise. They aren't in the thick of it. Amazing how several of them, when provided with a chance to become a hunter instead of a laborer, will not choose to be the hunter. Despite the fact that they will illicit opinions on how much a hunter should earn and what they should do with their earnings. The critic is not the person in the arena, to paraphrase Theodore Roosevelt. This is no different than when people slam single mothers, because they truly do not know the lengths that people, who have no parent or minimal support, while raising children, will go through simply to survive. It is a thankless job, but it also never pays off in the same financial sense as safety reigns supreme over risk-taking, for obvious reasons.

People love to criticize without actually looking at the engine underneath the hood of the car. They simply point to the car, size up what they believe is wrong with the car, then shrug it off as you obviously are stupid or greedy or something because you aren't doing it their way. Because they do not see all of the issues with the engine underneath the hood of the car. They do not measure what parts may cost to fix the engine, or what permits may be required to even service the vehicle, or anything else. To a critic, details are merely obstacles that they would rather not think about at all. They diagnose without the ability to engage, because that would cause too much effort, time, and brain power. Instead, they make a critical assessment with less data, through the framework of what they would have done instead, or what should be done as if their sweeping statement has any merit, and then they hold others accountable to making that occur. This is why the same group of voters who elect people who raise the taxes or the minimum wage, are also the same people who complain about prices going up. They cannot correlate that the two actions are cause and effect.

This is where a lack of marketing comes into play. Because people only think about what advertises to them, specifically. And what sells to them. And what turns them off. Instead of understanding that they do not have a role within the process beyond facilitating the sale. A lot of the software tech gurus make this mistake. They see manipulation through sales funnels as the core. Just another sales funnel, generates yet another sale. What they should ask: Do some of those sales funnels actually reduce interest in their product? But then again, I've never truly sold software, so me criticizing something that I do not know shows a shallowness to my own supposed depth in marketing and sales. Again, burn those fingertips, jump into the mix, then start to diagnose what can be improved.

Critics love to tell you the market as well. They grow into positions of power, often through distribution channels, then swear off anything you might know about the market. I had this issue with several distributor sales staff who refused to do a lot of business with me: Because they handled only a few hard cider options, and kept telling me how micro beer was the way to go. They didn't understand that my customers in The Cider Barrel were women, mainly 30-to-45, who liked as many varietal options as possible. When I looked over the distributor sales staff, they were always white men, with cargo shorts and a flipped back hat, who only pushed what they personally drank. So they didn't get my brand, or my customer. Yet they were more than happy to tell me who my customer needed to be, and why. I firmly believe this is why The Cider Barrel, under the new owner, failed. She listened to critics who pushed her to carry beer and other options. Not a good move. I wish her well back in Tennessee now that she has sold everything for scrap and gotten out of the lease, but it is a good lesson to those tempted. Ensure the critic knows what they are talking about prior to implementing their advice.

You will see this same phenomena when it comes to large special events. Sometimes, public fundraisers, where people will offer advice, unsolicited, on the spot to those managing the function. Never mind that none of these critics are grabbing a mop, or waiting until a post-event assessment of what went right, what went wrong. They want to provide "constructive criticism" on the spot, without much data beyond their own personal tastes. And they want you to accept it as the holy writ, without any true context as to why certain things, even what they wanted to have implemented, could not be done or was prevented by others from being done. Several good ideas are crushed by roadblocking petty people, who then will avoid accountability when others choose to call them out for it.

You can go absolutely crazy and broke trying to fulfill other people's laundry list of criticisms. And remember, they might not be customers simply because they criticize. Often, those who provide invalid complaints are not purchasing the product. They are doing the opposite, completely ensuring that no one purchases the product either. They want it their way, which is often free, or not at all. And they have no issue telling you how to do things better to suit solely them. I had this issue with The Cider Barrel when I first opened it. While it was great to have several packed houses, I would gain complaints that it was too small of a space, the lighting sucked, etc. I did take some of those criticisms to heart, did change some of the lighting to a softer light, but understood that the space size was never going to change.

Some criticisms do have validity, because they come from actual customers who had an issue but wanted to support the business. However, there was one little old lady who complained about everything, and if it didn't suit her, including the price of the product, she was willing to go to social media about it. Never mind that several of the product prices were for foreign export hard ciders which were not found within 100 miles of The Cider Barrel, as well as carried their own import / export taxes. She didn't care. I was wronging her simply by not accepting her criticisms as the holy writ, therefore, she was going to tear me apart online about it. We held a Cider Fest to support small businesses through a local Chamber nonprofit, and had a person flame us repeatedly online for the fact that we had event setup issues. Never mind that the tent company dumped off everything, but had no labor, so we used volunteers. And that we had several other cider companies back out at the last minute because of their own labor shortages in 2021. We still made a go of it, we raised $3,500 for charity, and the guy who criticized us up and down online didn't care, even though he got his money back. Some of the criticism offered on social media is about that user receiving their own validation. And then they go back to being their insignificant self.

I did another Cider Fest in 2022, thinking that I had perfected the model by having two young professionals of a veterinary clinic help. They didn't have a cent to their name. Instead, I fundraised the sponsorship to hold and underwrite the event. I promoted it through my store and other social channels. It was a hit, on a 100 degree day, but the misfortune was that the two women refused to pivot when needed. They made several mistakes, that I tried to correct on the fly, in order to improve customer satisfaction. Instead, they were all about the money. They saw everything that I did as "their money" therefore, they weren't going to reduce it, at all, in order to ensure customer satisfaction. They weren't the expert, but a form of the critic. They had someone else implement for them, they only saw what they wanted to see, and then, well, refused to do anything that the subject matter expert - myself - wanted to do. What a waste of energy. They got $15,000 out of the deal for their clinic, but another Cider Fest was out of the question entirely.

SMALL BUSINESS SCHOOL

Criticism comes from not actually doing something. Because when you have the time to critique something, you aren't trying to be loud about it. You generate other ideas as a flex to build off of what is there, not simply to tear down what isn't possible. I plainly didn't learn my lesson with the first group at Cider Fest, tried it again with another group, and found out that I wasn't good at dealing with the unrealistic expectations of others. So, I stopped doing it altogether. Sometimes, your ideas are not a reflection of what your implementation becomes.

UNCLE IRA AND THE MINNESOTA GOODBYE

What does this tell us in general about small business? That even at the top level, even at the level where you expect people to want to buy your product, there is still a fight to get them to actually purchase your product. Especially if they feel that you will offer your product to them for free. If your level of expertise is below theirs. Because it isn't about the product as much as who is offering it or at what availability it is being offered. Your goal is to not only fight the good fight, but understand what you are fighting.

In late December 2023, my uncle Ira died. He was a great guy, a Haida native from Alaska, and worked his entire life at the Boeing plant in Auburn. But he did not understand, fundamentally, until the day he died, that the "Minnesota goodbye" was real. His wife, my Aunt Maureen ("Aunt Mo"), was from Minnesota, as were her three sisters. Every holiday party, for over four decades, Ira would drive his wife and family over 40 miles down to Olympia, to meet with her sisters to celebrate. And at a certain point at night, my uncle Ira would get up, declare that it was time to go so they could make it home at a credible hour, and then wait... and wait... and wait... by the front door while my Aunt Mo would keep talking to her sisters. Her continual talking was part of the phenomena known as the "Minnesota goodbye," where a person's expected exit is continued to be extended out as the conversation never stops. And my uncle Ira never understood this lesson.

My uncle Ira was an intelligent man. He understood traffic and time, and the value of getting home so everyone could sleep accordingly. He had to work in the mornings. His wife had her own florist business. The kids had to go to school on time. And yet, that value never transcended the value of my Aunt Mo talking to her sisters. Despite the three women talking on the phone constantly throughout the gaps between the holiday visits.

"It's time to go, Maureen."

Uncle Ira would say this constantly. It became a joke enough that the kids, including their cousins (myself, my sisters), would wait for it, laugh and mimic him. Throughout his life, my uncle Ira thought that the value of what he was selling - getting home on time - superseded the conservation between three women which occurred almost weekly. He guessed the market wrong. Constantly. After he died, I envisioned that he likely is now standing next to the door after each holiday visit, waiting for his wife to join him. You can love the product and people that you are selling to, and still misunderstand how those buying that product are going to receive it being offered.

THE
SAPLING

"I still have mixed feelings about what growing up is - this thing that happens to everyone, so I've heard." - Taylor Swift

"Everything ends badly, otherwise, it wouldn't end." - 'Coghlan's Law' from the 1988 movie, "Cocktail."

THE SAPLING

It is at this point when you are expected to launch your small business. In whatever form it takes. Scary, isn't it? Thrilling? Of course. But still, the "yes, but..." guy is sitting on your shoulder, warning you of everything that could go wrong. But the risk-taker on your other shoulder is excited, ready to go. You have to measure out your ability between the two characters, ensuring that you have made the correct decision in the process. You are only a small tree at this point, a sapling. You are attempting to build up into a larger, stronger version of yourself in the forest of small business and in life. But it takes time, energy and a lot of sweat equity.

Regardless of your industry, you are expected to "Bring The Show" to every customer. We can chat all day about customer experience, but "The Show" is something different. There is an intangible nature to the spectacle. Some local idiot will refer to it as "cheesy." So what? If it brings people, it brings in dollars, it makes your profit & loss (P&L) green instead of red. Cheesy sells. Cheesy works. Cheesy is what someone without your bills to pay can call it, but if they were put directly into your shoes, they would either do cheesy, or they would have their business model go out like a fart in the wind.

I have seen a lot of people resist being cheesy. As if there are social brownie points available for those who hold themselves up to a "suit & tie" standard when it comes to consumer tastes and experiences. When I owned The Cider Barrel, I decided to do catering events, selling hard cider. I could have done so as everyone else did, through two taps in a cooler mechanism, known as a jockey box. Instead, I researched the matter online, discovered a place out of Michigan which did four taps per jockey box, then purchased a used van, puncturing eight holes for taps along the passenger side. Inside, I had 2-by-4s holding the entire keg system in place. There was also a speaker system, playing Van Halen's Panama, as I poured eight different hard cider combinations. All of it was part of "The Show."

None of it was really needed to carry out the pouring. But it was a conversation starter. I also renamed a lot of the hard cider combinations. Using a portable white board, I would rename "blackberry cider" to "Black Magic" or "winter melon" was renamed "White Walker Winter Melon" from Game of Thrones. None of this was truly needed. It literally changed nothing. But the names were eye-catchers. Conversation starters. The ability to get people to think, to try it, and in essence, move the hard cider as much as possible. When you disengage with your audience, they tune you out as well. This works for business owners who want to act too cool for school, who then claim that the customer didn't "get" their product. Really, it's you belittling your own shallow efforts. The customers saw through your bad marketing attempts and moved on. There's nothing really to be seen there. You told them that by putting a lack of effort into it.

The cider van was always a hit when I would take it out to special events. Guys would want to check out the back of it, see the handiwork inside. And women loved the various selections involved. Everything about "The Show" that made it cheesy also made it in demand. I didn't even paint the thing or spend additional funds on it. There were people who said something, that I needed to "brand" it, but they missed the point. The van's faded red paint wasn't what drew people to drink from it. The van was a resource of eight combinations when most cider vendors had 2-to-4, and it was a conversation starter with men who wanted to learn more about the van. And the van booked out for three summers, generating its own P&L far beyond what I could have imagined. All with a limited amount of ice and gas money spent.

You will get people who make various attempts to talk you into spending more than you have to, in order to bring "The Show" up to their standards. But really, "The Show" is about what the customer sees, not what someone who isn't paying anything wants to have happen. When I owned the semi-pro soccer team, it wasn't a massive amount of cost to pay $25 for two 8-foot-soccer balls that the attending kids could roll around on the field during half-time. No one was using the field, so why not? But it was "The Show" because it gave kids something to do. If you ever want to know what defines "fun," go ask a kid. Within five minutes, they will tell you if something is "fun" or not. And while semi-pro soccer played by college-aged students might be fun for five minutes, it is not enough to grab a crowd continually. Let alone a paid crowd of 350+ per event.

That is where bounce houses, e-Gaming trailers, and other activities such as playing music during the match began to occur. Because it is more "fun" than it is less "fun." We had our critics, mainly from rival soccer aficionados who were in their late-30s, and didn't understand why we would dare dismiss semi-pro soccer as something that was a carnival event in nature. As I was told by one of them as an insult, "take your bounce houses and start a fair." These groups played in front of crowds of 30, not 350, and were bewildered that having constant activities such as t-shirt cannons and other marketing aspects would be entertaining. The thing is, regardless of the event, you are a 2-hour window of passing the time. You choose how you are going to do it.

Whether it is in retail or any other business, you are still creating an event. You have to create an experience to where people want to buy-in, continuously. Those who act too cool for school do not get customers to pay for their entry, or buy their product. This is why movie theaters have gone bad. They aren't selling event experiences anymore. There are no roadshows, no ability to do something special that isn't available in the comfort of your own home. Sports have had the same issue, especially at the lower levels. Somewhere along the way, the people in charge decided that the last thing they want to do is create something unique or engaging. Instead, they just wanted to show off another stupid game, one similar to the 10,000 other games being played at the same time, around the world, reachable through any streaming platform.

Think about what movie theaters could be doing to enhance their films. Question and answer sessions with special guests. Or anything else that might trigger people to want to be a part of showing up to watch the film. Movie theaters have also reduced the enjoyment of the film. With commercials and previews, movies are now exhibited 30-to-40 minutes after the supposed scheduled showtime. Despite also selling reserved seating. So, if you are attempting to go on a date or simply have a night out away from the kids as a couple, you are essentially spending $20-to-$30 extra for a babysitter, simply to show up on time, only to have to sit through endless commercials. Along with the runtimes of films stretching more than two-and-a-half hours, this reduces the overall entertainment value proposition of the film exhibition itself. It would be far different if "The Show" was entertaining rather than merely advertising. Movie theaters have forgotten that, with the majority simply in business to sell extra food.

There is a similar thing happening in retail where there are long lines, limited supply of product, and the only urgency is to avoid it selling out in the first place. But if you can wait, and a lot of people can, you can order the product online and have it within a few days. There is no "Show" to speak of in most of the big box retail stores. No one who is an expert who can help you figure out your problems with a device, or to walk you through it. Apple Stores have defeated the online model, simply by being present, by having a Genius Bar where you can not only bring your item, but you can also have various issues sorted out in 15-to-30 minutes. Apple also does another whammy by simply having a better return policy. Unless you are a constant offender, Apple will believe you when the product doesn't work, take the return without a fight, and hand you a new product on the spot. This is part of "The Show" because it is unique enough in retail not to have a C.I.A. level of intimidating interview on whether you have the right receipt or not. Sure, there are examples of this not being the case with Apple, Inc., but those highlighted exceptions prove the rule.

As small business entrepreneurs, we forget who is the actual customer. You are not your customer. You are not purchasing the product. You were merely facilitating the ability for someone else to purchase the product. So you cannot be the wholly end result when it comes to how people choose to either buy or not buy your product from you, or the customer experience that they want. You can only help create "The Show" for the product to be best displayed to the customer to make that purchasing decision. Otherwise, you are an obstacle for the product, blocking the customer from knowing that they even may want to purchase it, by creating a lack of presentation for the product to stand out from all of the other items that the customer may otherwise choose to purchase.

We get confused over what our role is. We are paid to care. We are paid to be a part of the functionary which believes in the product that we are selling, distributing out to everyone. That confusion lands a lot of people in the poor house. They cannot believe that their product didn't sell the way that they wanted it to. The way that they envisioned it should. Because all they needed to see was the product, rather than "The Show" which illuminated the product into something magical. "The Show" creates that sense of urgency for the customer. Because the spotlight of "The Show" makes the product seem as if every customer is looking at it, all at once, and supplies might not last if the customer does not take action right now. There is a stark reason why engagement rings sell even more than wedding rings. Because if you don't put a ring on it, in anticipation of an entire ceremony with a larger ring on it, someone else will. For a while there, in religious communities, "promise rings" were a pre-cursor to engagement rings. Basically three rings to provide the same commitment status, because otherwise, that person gaining the commitment will find someone else to provide it.

Blaming the audience or customer base for not getting on board with a product is silliness and bad self-defensive mechanisms at play. Essentially, it is you as a marketer refusing to admit that you are not reading the market well. Or that you suck at your job. Too often, you can have an excuse or a paycheck. The consuming audience will speak to you loudly on what they do and do not want. It is up to you to decide to listen. Some people put their hands over their ears when the consumer starts to talk. Then they blame the consumer when no one buys what they have to sell. The market is the only opinion that matters. When you are selling the product, bringing "The Show" is your way of showing your response to what the market has to say and answering it in kind. Everything else is a form of malpractice.

Back to the family fun center that I owned back in 2019. It was closed in 2020 during the COVID-19 pandemic, and finally sold, moved up the road 30 miles to Tacoma, and opened in 2024. But despite all of the history of the place, it did not have the magic. The crowds didn't show up the same way that they did during the winters only 30 miles south of Tacoma, in Thurston County. That is because there are a multitude of things to do in Tacoma. There really isn't much, aside from some old mall territory, for kids to do, especially when it's raining, in Olympia. Part of being "The Show" is also knowing that your audience needs to buy in, because they have to give it a chance in the first place. If there are competing interests of fun, that is where it gets tough. The same goes for retail or any type of business. Think about the true aspects which change people's perception of something? It all comes down to presentation of "The Show."

Virgin Airlines was a remarkable way to travel. That is why other travel aircraft carriers killed it. Because Virgin Airlines didn't charge more for food or drinks. They had small plexiglass barriers between each row. And they had amazing lighting which made it feel like you were entering into a fun atmosphere of enjoyment. The flight attendants dressed a bit different, and everyone seemed happy. There was no beverage cart going down the aisle, or listening to people talk or babies cry. Virgin Airlines figured out how to bring "The Show" and they were so successful that their competitors found a way to manipulate Virgin's corporate board into selling the airline to Alaska Airlines, which promptly ended most of "The Show" in order to avoid their own airlines being faulty by comparison.

A lot of envy pushes destruction of brand. Sometimes, it is not the destruction of your own brand, but that of the brands that may get acquired, simply to avoid comparisons in the marketplace. When one brand buys another, they do not do so by adopting any of the innovations that the acquired brand illustrated. Instead, they do the opposite. They murder that brand worst than Caesar's death, a thousand knives coming from every direction. Because, why would a brand purchasing another, actually feel that the competitor they purchased had any actual innovation? This is where brands go off-scale and end up hurting themselves in the long-run.

This comes back to the family fun center. It didn't really present anything different than what it originally had, but the audience is also different 30 miles away. This is a confounding principle that most people refuse to engage with: Your audiences are not the same in every location. Even if you decide to have a franchised business, it needs to adapt with the area and the times. Otherwise, you are finding a greater issue: Mislabeling your audience overall. And with the family fun center, their revenues were crap because 30 miles away in Tacoma, they had several competitors fighting for that same dollar. In Olympia, they had zero competitors, which made them the best deal in town.

We are faced with these challenges in our lives at certain points. Sometimes, it comes with the benefits of an idea that sparks us enough to solve a problem. Or it can be an opportunity for reputation destruction. For every entrepreneur, the idea will not be enough. It will be the germ. It will stay there until an opportunity presents itself. Sometimes, you have no choice in the matter. At the start of every opportunity is the end of another one. In the early summer of 2001, I was working at OCLC, a nonprofit database center in Lacey, Washington. A $200 million nonprofit that hired me, along with a staff of seven, to sit in our cubicles and manually type library cards into the system. All day, every day. It was a good job, it paid decent, and did not require more education than typing 50 words per minute. And then, one day, it ended badly.

All seven of the OCLC employees were asked to leave our cubicles. We were brought into the meeting room, and summarily laid off from the nonprofit company. The issue was that the Ohio company could not wrap their brains around a Washington state law, which allowed for two 15 minute breaks per eight hour shift. Despite being a nonprofit, OCLC made a corporate level decision to pack up its wares and relocate the entire operation to Ohio, where they could be free of the two 15 minute break legal mandate of Washington state.

Shocked, each laid off staff member was provided with three months of severance pay, their vacation, and sick leave, all in a large check. As we exited the conference room, the laid off seven were witness to our cubicle being torn down by a NASCAR level pit crew of handymen. The walls were coming down in record time, and our things were packed into a box, set aside from the mess, for us to take. I was told at the time that this was all part of growing up. I was 25, out of work in a growingly bad 2001 economy (9/11 was only a few months away) and unsure what to do with my life. Every entrepreneur gets hit with this realization when the paychecks aren't automatic to their accounts every 10th and 25th of the month. When they really have a grasp of knowing, there is no turning back now.

Everything comes down to mindset. You can either get stuck or get moving. Whether you decide to leave your job, get laid off, get fired or forced into remote work, it is easy to fall in a trap of complacency. Because there are less expectations on you. The same issues exist in small business. When less is expected in certain areas, you cut corners of efficiency. Break that mentality by getting up the same time each morning. Take a shower. Dress as if you are going to work. Then be very active. Set appointments throughout the day. Find activities in the community. Learn. Engage. Keep your mind active. Young stay-at-home mothers face this issue. They were once involved in the world, then they remove themselves from the world to take care of their child or children. The issue is that they get removed from mental stimulation and need to find ways to keep their minds active. Long term, it hurts them, along with the children, if they do not seek out active resources of mental activity.

You always have the choice about what to do. Generally, people do not take that choice to start a small business. They often return to education or find another job. It is difficult to cash in your pension or Roth IRA to fund a business. Especially if you have a family. Regardless of whether you have a business model that is functional or not, having a family means many mouths to feed. Having a small business is about sacrifice more than anything. But there are some cases where you shouldn't necessarily take the easy reward over the risky small business. That's a choice that some people refuse to accept. I went the college route, earning three degrees in six years, starting at community college. I still understood that everything is sales. If you hate sales, you are truly against living, as everything, including your own identity, is about selling yourself to others. What do you think a cover letter and resume are for a company's hiring committee? Sales. Yet, people think they are taking less risk by working for someone else instead of for themselves.

Generations are always faced with uncertainty and different points in the road. The Roaring 20's had a generation built on luxury and living on margin. The Great Depression taught generations not to spend anything at all. To save every penny. To avoid debt at all cost. By the end of the 1940's, generations were borrowing again, creating a gigantic economic boom which would last until the early 1970's. Then the economies were cyclical, going from boom to near bust, including the crashes of 1987, 2002, and 2008. Yet, less than 90 years past the lessons of The Great Depression, consumer debt hit over $17 trillion. That's over $100,000 per household. The idea of knowing how to go out on your own in the new economy is irrelevant if you do not know how to live below the means of "The Joneses."

An entrepreneur is built on survival instinct. They do not buy houses that are not paid off completely. They do not have education or car loan debt. And they certainly do not add more children to the mix. The idea of having what someone else has, simply to impress someone, is not sustainable for the entrepreneur. Everything is about saving, understanding, and gaining traction toward not only owning a business, but having a business that will survive. It is also who the entrepreneur surrounds themselves with that matters as well. Surround yourself with those who are also in a survival mode, not a buy mode. Do not compare yourself to those who inherited their wealth or business, whose grandparents selected their line of work long before the third or fourth generation was even born. As Mark Twain once wrote, "comparison is the thief of joy."

Ask yourself what you are spending on that doesn't need to be purchased. Is this product necessary to attract multiple customers to buy it? Is this item built for the customer experience, or for my own personal taste or ego? Can I get it cheaper without people knowing what I paid for it? The Cider Barrel walls were covered in $200 total of reclaimed fencepost, stained with $25 of industrial vinegar and sanded down, then vacuumed. The people who entered the bar thought that I spent far more than that. If 2-by-4s bought at Home Depot, that are also burned by a blow torch and then stained, achieve the goal of a priceless customer presentation, shouldn't that be the overall goal? When I owned my video company, I bought a 10-year-old Canon 7D Mark ii camera used for $750. I have used it through 2025 for various gigs. While I have had some upgrades, that camera has more than recouped its investment about 100 times over. And it was never the latest model of camera that offered 1/100th more depth of field or something that only a video snob might notice.

You should also recognize whether the safety net of receiving a paycheck each monthly from someone else is worth more or less what you would receive otherwise. This is the hardest equation to calculate, since it depends on you, your unique situation, and whether you can make more simply by working for yourself doing the same job as you would if working for someone else. The malarky of merely "doing your passion" does not always equate to a sustainable independent job. Look into the past, there were people who immigrated to this country with little to nothing, didn't even speak the language, and built up an empire. Sometimes laundromats or dry cleaning or barber shops. Doubtful that they were following their "passion" as much as earning more than they would working for someone else.

We tend to receive information from the wrong sources speaking to us through media. Those who seem to be independent, but clearly aren't. Movie actors talk up the values of socialism or equal pay, while not being an independent contractor themselves. They receive residual checks for their work from an employer, a movie studio, and tend to go on strike anytime they feel their contract is undercut. They also aren't paying for other workers, therefore they exist in the bubble of thinking they know what something costs, rather than knowing truly what something costs. And then they put out material which paints every business leader as an evil capitalist, while benefiting from that source of economic development.

Even those movie actors aren't espousing the idea of themselves financing and producing their own movies. Despite this being the case back in 1919, with D.W. Griffith, Charlie Chaplin, Mary Pickford, and Douglas Fairbanks forming United Artists. They financed their own films, asserted creative control, this was to be a worker's dream come true. However, United Artists didn't sell public stock as the other studios did, produced only five films per year, and by 1933, was organized for what would be a million times until its 1981 sale to MGM for $350 million. Turns out that artists like to be artists and let the details be handled by someone else. All of the originating founding stars dropped out of the UA deal, determining that it was better to receive a wage, rather than be an entrepreneur.

ENTREPRENEUR OR WAGE SLAVE

This is a choice that you have to make. No one can make it for you. Either you want to take a chance on yourself, or you desire to earn a wage. There's nothing wrong with the wage component, but realize that while the risk is lower, the reward is non-existent. Wages equal out that there is a guarantee against your timed labor, but that you are at the mercy of others in order to be promoted or paid more. You are a slave to other's aspirations. You are not free to do what you wish with the window of time that you have. If you don't want to think, if you merely want to earn a certain amount, then you are desiring to be a wage slave. You may also have to pay into a union in order to protect your job. So, you're paying for the right to keep working at a lower rate because you cannot trust yourself to risk anything and everything on your own dreams or aspirations.

I encounter this phenomena a couple of times each year. One of my issues is that I get invested in the excitement of helping others attempt to achieve their goals. What I learn from this is that the majority, and I mean the vast majority, aren't cut out to risk or bet on themselves. In fact, it is the opposite. And they want my help, but only to then push back after I've made an investment in them, because, well, they suck. Not only do they suck, but they have horrible people around them. Usually parents or dimwitted friends. People who they have placed in their circle who are not capable of betting on themselves, and who see it as a sinister or misguided act that their child or friend bet on themselves when clearly they haven't done so themselves. That's a weird sentence, I understand, but it does come down to the investment level that someone is willing to have in themselves, or the investment level that they are willing to allow their loved ones to have as well.

I posit the question of entrepreneur or wage slave simply to point out that not everyone or the majority of folks aren't willing to be entrepreneurs. Recently, I attempted to help a 22-year-old who was earning $1,000 a month in take home pay, who had worked for multiple cleaning companies, including a rundown motel where she was cleaning 68 rooms a day. I broke down all of the per square footage rates for charging, we catalogued cleaning products and needs, and even found her an office to hold all of the supplies. I even brought her to a local chamber event, where she immediately had eager commercial customers willing to hire her. She couldn't handle it. She sent me a text message the size of a novel, on how she couldn't handle the stress or risk of starting her own business. She was comfortable being a wage slave, not an entrepreneur.

She would have generated close to $12,000 a month gross, $8,500 a month net as an entrepreneur, compared to the $1,000 net that she received as an employee. But she couldn't handle it. Some people are conditioned to be wage slaves, regardless of the size of the chain around their neck. So, she will continue to clean 68 rooms that are 16 square feet by 20 square feet (320 total square feet) for 5 nights a week, earning $1,000 monthly. At the $0.17 per square foot model that we calculated for her business, that would have been $54 per room, or $3,699 each night, or $18,496 per 5 days, or $73,984 per month. Instead, she will earn $1,000 monthly to do 6,400 square feet a month worth of cleaning. Essentially, to be a wage slave at $14.49 minimum wage per hour for the State of Washington in 2020, she was losing a ton of money because of the "safety" of an hourly wage.

These wages were built in a different era. Where people couldn't do multiple jobs at once, especially passive income where online sales generate capital. It has also been conditioned into people to demand their own safety net when it comes to earning potential. They refuse to engage or understand with the belief that they can earn more money simply by creating new revenue streams. They see the gross revenue, but they shirk at the overall net gain because they cannot wrap their brain around it. This is why you have to create a choice for yourself. Are you an entrepreneur? Are you merely a wage slave? Even if you're not the overall entrepreneur and you're around someone that is, are you a supportive person or a dream killer? It all factors into the decision to keep reading further.

I have nothing against working for someone else. I've done it. Others have done it. I can respect it. But this book series is not about working for other people. It is about accountability to yourself. Understanding that you have a larger value and purpose. But a lot of people will close their mind off to that purpose. Depends on whether you want to be an assistant manager at someone else's salon or run your own salon instead. Sure, there's a lot of risk to running your own salon. But that comes with removing the chain around your neck. Some folks cannot handle it. They see it as an affront overall.

That young woman that I tried to help? Well, she backed out because there were business cards made and things "moved too fast." She felt that she needed to get an education first, formally, through college, rather than do something that she had already been trained in. So she needed to have debt from a degree, to do cleaning, which anyone could do. This is part of that overall conditioning by others. How she thought she would earn that degree, while generating $1,000 a month, was beyond me. Some people you have to allow to make their own decisions, and if those decisions don't jive with yours, then you have to leave them behind. The worst thing that you can do is keep low-hanging fruit people or negative people within your realm. It's not worth it. They are excuse makers, not entrepreneurs. They deserve the lack of freedom that they crave.

Chances are, she will be at the bottom of the employment pool for the remainder of her life, earning either at minimum wage or just above it. Because she didn't believe enough in herself to become an entrepreneur. Always be aware that there are an active political group of people who believe that you are only as good as the slowest person on the planet.

They re-enforce that belief in the idea that you should be taxed out of your realistic earnings as an entrepreneur because it helps those who didn't bet on themselves at all. And then they give it to people like the cleaning woman, who chooses not to take your path, where it keeps the chain around her neck a little tighter, where she doesn't even realize she's a slave until it's too late. The choice is yours in how you want to proceed.

She is not alone. People retain insight or knowledge into a subject because they've worked it, yet see the knowledge as worthless. The laundromat where I had one of my candy machines had a teenager named Bonnie. While chatting with her, she broke down every component of each laundromat machine. From wash to dry. Which parts needed to be replaced, how long cycles went through, and whether certain loads of laundry were worth more than others to the business. Yet, despite working at that laundromat for three years, Bonnie decided to move to another state and work at a gas station. She had all of the components to be a laundromat consultant but did not see that knowledge as something other people would pay to have when opening or operating their own laundry facility. This type of behavior occurs more than you think.

Entrepreneurs in one area of business will commit the art of seppuku in another. Seppuku is the Japanese ritual act of suicide, by stabbing yourself with a sword or blade. There was a local entrepreneur who made his original fortune with office furniture for state offices. Did quite well. Expanded into office supplies. Then, when office furniture sales lagged, his office supplies line took off. That entrepreneur was dismayed and told me that he was a "furniture guy." He worried more about what his neighbors would say if they learned he made a lot of his new business on "toilet paper." Sometimes, people lack the ability to accept what they can build a fortune off of. They are too concerned with the image over the substance. That is when they fail.

We count on things way too often, without knowing that they could end at any time. In college, my class had a guest speaker who was a Hollywood puppeteer in the 1990s. He was in demand constantly, worked on major films, won several industry awards, and finally felt comfortable to take a two week vacation and avoided certain films because digital animation was taking off. He refused to learn new technology because he was a traditionalist into the art of puppeteering. Because of his two week absence, he missed out on pitching his services to three major films requiring puppeteering. He mentioned that after his two week vacation ended, he ended up being out of work for over two years from a lack of work.

SMALL BUSINESS SCHOOL

LEARN TO PIVOT

Everyone needs to know how to pivot in their business structure. Every business needs this. But yet, several business types die because they refuse to pivot. They get stuck. They see business as only one process, not several moving parts. And when immediate or gradual change happens, they freeze or get caught up in the issue of not knowing how to change. Everything is fluid, moving as parts do, and if you don't move and pivot as new issues come at you, then the business model you have slows to a halt and eventually dies. Film cameras were eaten alive by digital cameras, which were eaten alive by smart phones. Technology and trends change. And business is an adapt or die situation.

COVID-19 shutdowns in states have been a perfect example of this. If you had a restaurant without delivery, or without online ordering technology, then you got absolutely killed. If you fought the delivery apps, or if you didn't push online advertisements, you didn't make sales. And even then, your service was questioned. What you were doing in January 2020 was different by March 2020, and the world changed forever. It calls into question what pivoting you could do, and how creative you could be. The lesson is to never get stuck in one solo type of operation, expecting it to never change. Because change is constant.

The lesson out of COVID-19 and states shutting down for small business is that you can be shut down at any time. For any reason. You have to know how to create new business structures in order to avoid that. And expecting the government to react, within a specific amount of time, especially when it comes to rebating or creating a recoupment of income for the lost income or customers that you have, is rather foolish. Government structure and processes are slow to react to anything. That is the form of government in a nutshell, even if you believe fully in the socialist structure of government. They have too many layers of bureaucracy to react efficiently, because they need input from too many resources. Whereas in business, you can pivot immediately with the ability of one or two decision-makers' approval to a plan.

Make no mistake about your business, you are in the business to make money. It sounds silly, but several small business owners, when faced with a crisis, will yield their strength of making money or making a large, impactful decision, on the basis that they are "not in this to make money." That is a defense mechanism. It is about encountering pride more than logic. And you cannot reason with those types of business owners, who would rather go into debt or destruction of their business, rather than yield their current business model to a business model that actually might work. When faced with the issue of a dying business model, as an entrepreneur, you either react or you die, simple as that.

Everything is about seeing what the market can bear. Then do it. If the market says that your one business doesn't work in its current form, but allows you another form in which to do business, then you must switch up. I was in the bar business until COVID-19 caused shutdowns, but I switched over to selling retail of the canned alcohol products, because I could stay open. It allowed me to learn most about my customers, about what they want, what they will pay to obtain, and I generated money until my bar could be open again. And it also created another product vertical for me to sell, allowing me more revenue generation on-top of what I already had. That's because I chose to pivot, while the other bars in my small town folded or closed up or spend thousands monthly on tents and heaters in the dead of winter, trying to stay open.

You have to engage with customer volume in relation to product turn-over. In selling candy, I placed all of my machines out in different places. One of them was a car stereo installer's company lobby. It didn't pan out as a place where kids sat with quarters, waiting to eat candy. And the candy machine was dead for most of the year that it was there. I learned from that process that simply placing a distribution channel somewhere does not mean that it will suddenly be used. And in fact, the candy sitting in that machine went bad, had to be thrown out. So effectively, I paid for a lesson. Without failure, there is no ability to learn how to be successful.

Being stuck means that you aren't making money. You have to see what you can do without, cut where you can, expand in order places that generate money, and go from there. Nothing exists in a vacuum. Everything is about pivot, pivot, pivot when it comes to small business. The moment you stop adapting, you are dying. The customer sees that too. They want to help a sob story only so much. You need to make yourself a necessary brand that they want to align with. Something that they will always buy from, because you have what they need, and you know how to pivot when the market changes.

And there were a lot of folks who played it safe prior to the COVID-19 pandemic. They sat in their safe jobs working for someone else. Then they were laid off, forced to work remote, then fell into a cyclical trap. You should always be growing, regardless of your job field. You should always have multiple plates spinning at all times, because if one fails, you will have another that replaces it. Adventure means constant stimulation through exciting initiative. Some people won't get the thrill, others will mock your "lack of time." But the thing is, if you put out different components constantly far enough in advance, you have more time than you know what to do with.

There are multiple sources of personal and professional development to gain knowledge from. This book is a great primer, but should not be the sole source. But thank you for the royalty I will receive for your purchase of this book. I would recommend that you constantly build, form new ideas, listen to audio books in the car, in spare minutes. Learn over time. Gain information constantly. Evolve into a better sense of yourself. What value are you adding to the lives of your customers through your business? What can you do in advance to avoid preventable issues in your small business later on?

EASTMAN KODAK, BORDERS BOOKS, & NY PUBLISHING

Every business school will have a class study on Eastman Kodak. Once the ruler of photographs, it pioneered photography development and technology. It made the amateur photographer an important part of its business model. Eastman Kodak simplified film processing for the consumer. The company was unstoppable, considered one of the most successful businesses in the world. But it could not pivot when technology changed and became the cautionary tale for business professionals. When you do not adapt, you die. Even if it's 100 years after dominating the marketplace. Eastman Kodak was slow to respond to digital photography in the 1990s and 2000s. It did not foresee or grasp the adaptability of changes to amateur photography, including the launch of the iPhone which essentially put photography on an entirely different level. No longer did you carry a camera around with you separate from your phone.

Borders Books & Music did not pivot despite having several hundred stores by 2001. It was a retail juggernaut. A giant in its field. They created an internet book-selling venture with Amazon, providing Amazon with Borders customer list. Amazon took over Borders.com and Borders refused to sell its books online. When customers walked into a Borders store, they were often directed to search Amazon to order the product. Borders killed its $1.6 billion dollar business by refusing to pivot, dead by 2011 with an entire liquidation. In Japan, there is the form of ritualistic suicide known as seppuku, where the act consists of oneself stabbing into their own abdomen with a short sword to ensure an agonizing, slow death. Borders provided a business version of seppuku through the Amazon deal, which did not benefit their company at all and ended with its slow, agonizing demise only a decade later.

Amazon did benefit the consumer and the writer in an area where traditional publishing did not. You are reading this book or listening to this audiobook, because of that benefit. Until the mid-2000s, if any writer chose to be self-published, it was called "vanity publishing" and disregarded as non-serious content. The New York publishing houses made determinations about what the reader wanted. Few if any times would a book on "small business" be considered, let alone be publishable. It would have not sold enough books to make the entire publication worthwhile. Amazon changed that with its 2007 purchase of Create Space, opening up the ability to register for an ISBN (library tracking number) and print-on-demand publishing services when someone ordered a book off of Amazon.

The New York publishing houses still have not pivoted from this issue. They are dying quails that refuse to believe that you, the consumer, would read something that wasn't published by one of their deemed "sanctioned" writers. And yet, you are. Millions of people are within the Amazon print-on-demand space. It grows because consumer demand is now much more niche. People want specific things, and the New York publishing houses did not and still refuse to provide it. All of it comes down to local control, offering something that benefits the consumer, which the larger publishing houses refuse, or cannot imagine, should be offered in the first place. Their loss.

TROY KIRBY

FINDING YOUR TARGET MARKET

Target markets are everywhere. Everything is less a shotgun approach compared to a rifle shot. Hitting the absolute target, and knowing who you are trying to sell to. That means limiting your customer base to a specific line goal, in order to absolutely attract it. You need to have a specific knowledge of who would buy your product and why they would be attracted to it. You cannot drive sales by not knowing who specifically would buy it. Let's suggest that you are selling wigs; you cannot sell wigs to people with long, flowing hair. At least not on a regular basis. Perhaps as a novelty, but then that likely suggests that you are selling around a specific theme or holiday, such as Halloween, where dressing up in costume is part of the action. That's why knowing your target market and hitting it becomes so important.

So, who are you exactly selling to? Why do you feel that they need your product? Why do they absolutely require your product in order to exist in the world? Entertainment is as much of a need as food in some worlds. In other worlds, entertainment is the last thing that someone requires, when all they want is food. You have to know what exists and what is needed and what is required within the sphere of influence and the hierarchy of needs for your target market. Every audience is different, so is every sphere of influence, as well as what they require to function. This is something that you need to know when focusing on your target marketing – how much do they really need, i.e. really require, your product in their lives? If you misjudge a target market, you may be sitting around with zero sales for a long period of time.

These groups drop down into specific categories of need. And that means asking why these groups have formed. Are they consistent groups? Are they merely passive or fad groups, where they aren't really interested in consuming or purchasing your product long-term? Are you going to be able to deliver that product to that target market enough, even when you start having competitors appear? And finally, why have you selected that target market group in order to sell to? It may not be a sufficient target market to focus on, in order to continually sell your product. If you cannot achieve sales on a consistent basis from that target market, is it actually harming the amount of revenue or sales goals that you could be achieving by focusing on a different target market? All of this depends on whether you feel that the target market is worth it at all.

In order to really engage with a product's target market, you need to focus on three or four that can be hit at different times, for different reasons, at the same time. This allows you to draw from multiple audiences at once, engaging them in multiple ways, and always ensuring that you have a good base to sell to. Starbucks Coffee isn't selling solely coffee. It's always selling a space to do homework and meet up for business deals, with its Wi-Fi and comfy chairs. It is also selling different "third place" functions, such as light breakfast sandwiches and blueberry muffins, as well as a good place to host small public events. Imagine if Starbucks didn't focus on anything but the true coffee latte crowd; all it takes is people to be turned off by coffee for Starbucks to be out of retail space. Instead, by having multiple things going on at once, to multiple target markets, Starbucks makes itself sustainable against fads and breaks in their revenue categories. This is how Starbucks survives and thrives, by always being a different target market experience to everyone who walks through the door.

This also points out that there is no true target market to sell to. Selling to one target market solely is business suicide. It positions your entire product to be sold to one small audience. And that audience often, because they are tribal in their concern, attempts to isolate out other potential target markets from joining. That is what people do.

Tribal politics exists no matter how many groups will attempt to allow inclusion, they will always deny membership to new candidates based on the idea of a loss of equity in the product. That is why you have to cater to multiple target markets at once. Otherwise, if people see themselves as your sole source of income, they will not allow you to thrive, instead closing off your potential revenue for their own tribal gain.

Avoid the idea of the best target market to sell to. You want to have these target markets competing for your product's attention. This is one of my arguments against The Sports Clips model; which purposely sells to the idea of "sports bar guys" purchasing haircuts. While that may seem like a good target market audience, with the TVs blaring the NFL Network on a Tuesday afternoon where there are no games being played, it also forgets that a lot of people who want haircuts and are willing to pay $35, aren't really sports fans. They dress their hair stylists like referees, but none of those cutting hair tend to know anything about sports. They don't do the little dirty work of stats regurgitation to their customers. And they tend to avoid looking at the other target markets available, such as selling to small children haircuts, by not having a separate pricing structure. This is where Sports Clips has a failing model, in my opinion, because it doesn't try to be flexible to other target markets and instead caters specifically to the "sports bar guys" target market solely.

Then it comes down to learning from that target market itself. Everything is about creating an opportunity to learn what your target market can teach you about itself. What are its likes, dislikes and the things that you are irrationally stereotyping about that target market which are actually untrue. People are contradictions. People say one thing, do another. Because they don't like the imagery projected on a subject or mannerism, they will instead do the opposite or suggest the opposite. This means that you have to learn not only from what that target market thinks about itself, but the purchasing data and other patterns of revenue generation which may state the opposite.

I know a local country singer who created an image for her fans of being heartbroken and single. I learned later that she had been married to the band guitarist for years. All of her songs about being catfished by a married man, well, who knows what the truth is? But once you realize that she is fraudulently hitting a target market who identifies with her, I think it cheapens the customer experience with her music. There is a falseness there, suggesting that you are a fool to believe in being connected to her music.

That is why if you sell to a target market, you must believe in the customers buying into that concept. There's a coffee shop that is focused on the van camping mentality, but they are former van campers themselves. Same with "The Chocolate Man" who has a small Mountlake Terrace shop outside of Washington. He not only teaches chocolate at one of the local community colleges, he also sources chocolate from all over the world. There is a wide gap between merely selling crap to a target market and actually living out the things that you sell that help a customer experience the product better.

From that point, it becomes a continual learning and updating of your business plan on how to target these consumers, as well as the patterns, which may be forever changing. As a business entrepreneur, you need to be focused on continual learning. Not just from those who have business advice, but also from your consumers and the data that pulls from it. If you can learn from your competitors' customers, prior to investing in actual infrastructure, then all the better. But if you need to start-up your business, that means looking back on the data of any customers you have. You need to see where customer movement has changed. And it will – nothing stays the same – technology can also be a large part of this change – and you need to be able to react to those changes.

Simply put: Finding your target market doesn't mean that you won't continually fight to keep and relearn how your target market evolves. You will be under a constant threat of losing your target market, and left out in the cold in the process. SEARS-Roebuck had generated 1-percent of the gross domestic product (GDP) of the United States in 1972. By 1978, they were almost bankrupt. They restored themselves several times, in the 1980s and 1990s, by examining and re-examining their target market. But by the late 2010s, they were taken into bankruptcy and killed for good. Even for a 100-year-old company that has seen it all, has the investors and the supposed experts to protect its bottom line, the lack of education on an evolving target market can be a downfall. They didn't see Amazon, Apple, Microsoft and Google coming in their rearview mirror, losing all of those target markets over time. As of 2023, Apple is valued at 10% of the entire U.S. GDP, with a market cap of $2 trillion dollars. Amazon, Microsoft and Google are listed at $1 trillion dollar market caps. Imagine how hard the fall may be when one or two of these digital companies collapse. SEARS-Roebuck didn't see it coming and folks in 1978 would have scoffed at the idea. 'At first it was gradual, then it was sudden,' as Hemingway wrote in his 1926 novel, The Sun Also Rises. Losing a target market is no different than losing your personal fortune.

WHAT IS THE NEIGHBORHOOD LIKE?

Whenever I hear a small business start-up pitch, I am quick to ask about the neighborhood the store or warehouse will be located in. Not what foot traffic is like. But whether the neighborhood is welcoming to the business. This may sound strange, but not every neighborhood is the same. Every neighborhood is also not a downtown. And this conversation has little to do with the lease and more to do with the neighboring businesses along with the clientele they attract.

An entrepreneur settling on locations to run a start-up needs to have three options to lease. Not just one. Sorting out the details with the landlord is only after you investigate the neighborhood itself. Walk into the local shops. See what the area is like after dark. Do the police respond to calls at night? Are there people screaming and carrying on at a local dive bar a block down? Are there vagrants or criminals lurking, trying to key or steal cars? What is the parking situation like, not just for your customers, but also for your employees? All of these things should factor into your decision to lease a location. Along with finding out who your retail and warehouse neighbors are.

You should be concerned about locating near co-ops or left wing coffee shops. Face it, every great coffee shop is left wing. But it's whether the coffee shop is run by left wing hippies or left wing violent extremists that should concern you. Left wing hippies aren't going to burn dumpsters, break windows and attract the worst element possible around their premises. When you sign a lease and open your business, you are investing in the community itself. Your responsibility also hinges on your investment in the safety of your customers, who are traveling from other locations to see you. This is why shopping malls and strip mall outlets typically get a lot of small businesses. They are private property with paid security and can trespass any vagrant who is causing trouble.

It is important to know who your neighbors are, what they support and do not support, and whether they will be supportive of your business. "Some people just want to watch the world burn," Alfred The Butler says in the 2008 film, The Dark Knight. The same can be said about some of the businesses around your potential location. Some folks simply worked for a state agency, retired, and spent a little from their retirement so they would have a job. And they call themselves an entrepreneur, going from home to store, with zero interest in actually generating a profit. Having something to do is more than enough for them.

It matters that you realize this in advance of whom you invest around. They could either bring in good customers or negative elements. And you may be stuck with an unbreakable lease, a five year commercial with a three percent annual hike in year, with no way to get out of it. Never walk down the aisle with a person you saw from across the bar but never had a conversation with. Investigate who these folks are prior to investing in them or the area itself. That location may be more trouble than it's worth.

That co-op restaurant ended up finally folding at the end of 2024. All resulting from the permits, fees and bureaucracy that its members had advocated and voted for. No one thinks that the taxation and penalties and bureaucracy will affect them. But the thing about creating the hydra is that once the multiple dragon heads are born, the less likely you are to be able to control them from snapping and breathing fire on you. Similar to a larger business creating Human Resources policies, the growth of that monster becomes uncontrollable and everyone, including the head of the organization, is fair game.

THE WINE SNOB COMETH

I had a good conversation with a wine snob who owned a local wine shop who didn't investigate his location enough. He was worried. He deemed that too many new competitors were coming into the marketplace around him. Turns out, his landlord owned a majority of the retail buildings around the area and was leasing to anybody, including the wine snob's competitors. Too many wine shops were starting up. Too many new wine bars right around the corner. Sure, he was busy during the last year, but he was worried all the same. And I asked him why he was worried. He shook his head, telling me that those folks could buy more volume than he could. Then they would discount him out of the marketplace. Honestly, I wanted to tell him that the only thing that the wine snob was discounting was his own expertise, which would win out where it counted every time. I refrained.

Regardless of your business, pricing your products happens to be one of the most aggravating or fulfilling segments of energy that you will ever undertake. It is either a debit or a credit on the balance sheet. You decide how much. And that's where the rub is; ensuring that you are not charging too little or too much for customers in search of a fair price. Every business is different. Two businesses, side by side, may charge different prices for the same product, based on the experience that they are providing to their customers. The first business may charge a 1.5 times that of wholesale, simply because the product isn't within the total line of their customer value. The second business may charge 5.5 times that of wholesale for the same product that the first business also offers, but may also provide a larger experience as a result. And the second business may end up selling more of that product, at a higher premium, because their customers value that product more and do not price shop at the next store over.

This is why charging the least amount for your product is not good business. Let the coupon hunters discover the cheaper version. That may be the only interest they have overall; discovering a good deal. While a lot of business owners attempt to attract these customers for their revenue frequency, it is actually a wrong-headed focus on getting small amounts of transactions not worthy of your time. Filling up a retail establishment with 100 customers may sound great, but if those 100 customers each spend $10 each on a bottom-rate deal which provides a net profit of $3 per transaction, that isn't really a winner. That's $300 in net profit after spending $700 in product procurement. If 50 customers are willing to spend $25 for that same product, earning the business $18 per transaction, that's $900 in net profit against $700, which makes the investment much more attractive. It's whether you decide to attract a higher-end client base, or cheap customers, on a frequency basis, that matters entirely.

When you first get a wholesale product, your intention is to sell it for a profit. Obviously. But how much should your wholesale product be offered up for at the retail price? Anywhere from 2.5 times to 6.5 times of wholesale price is a good rule of thumb. Let's say that it is a $10 wholesale item. At 2.5 times, it equals out to $25. At 6.5 times, it arrives at a retail price of $65. If you are charging a 65% net profit margin, you have to ask yourself if you can get it. You likely can get it at the lower end, as mentioned, with discount hunters. However, when you do this, your lower price becomes your price. It is hard to move that price up. But if you have an asking price at 65% net profit margin, you can also turn away even good spending customers who feel that your price is inflated and way too high for the asking.

This comes to the idea of experience being a factor in what you price your product at. When someone enters your store or your online space, are they looking for that specific product that fits their needs, etc.? Is there more of an exclusivity to what you are selling than your competitors? Do you carry more of the product or product types than anyone else? All of these factor into the decision-making process of what you price your products at. How much inventory you are carrying, as well as how much time it takes to sell through that inventory, also factors into the overall decision. Especially if that inventory has a set expiration date. There are a lot of variables when you price your product.

A lot of this comes down to the idea of knowing the business of your business. There are a lot of people who have decided to shut off their minds to knowing their numbers, or knowing how to generate sales or pivot their business effectively. The problem is that once you do that, you lay victim to passive business behavior. The idea that once the spout shuts off, you won't be able to dig a new well, instead, you'll just let the entire thing dry up around you. That's why knowing the business of your business matters.

The wine snob will be fine. He will host several wine club parties and get a re-investment of his business from his customers. His competitors are not as versed in wine as he is. They are not experts in the room. People often mistake the idea that a discount can kill an expert business. But if given the choice, would you rather have a burger at McDonald's or one at a fine restaurant. Sure, the McDonald's one may be cheaper, but you know it's poorly made by comparison of the fine restaurant, which is why you pay more at the fine restaurant. Price also equals value when it showcases the expertise and skill behind it. And people always pay for value over buying crap, even if it's more expensive. The same can be said if you are a local business. People understand things cost more when it comes from local artisans, because they aren't undercutting the people making it.

LOCAL BRANDS SELL MORE

When you sell something that is local, you can get people to care about it, specifically because it has a local feel to it. And the expertise shows from those selling it. Usually a business of one or two. But the heart is there in what they are selling. To the consumer, that also means generally that they know where the product's revenue is going to go; i.e. back into their community. It doesn't even have to be a lot of money, but it can make an impact. People will always support local. Generally, they see you on the street, or in their church, or at their local restaurant. They see you in the neighborhood, and they want to support that. As more time passes, the impact of purchasing from someone making or selling a local product is actually greater. Because it means more. When you are local and selling, people tend to care.

When people love the area, that relationship comes back to those who sell in that area, especially if they are selling area (i.e. local) stuff. Whether it has the name of the city on a t-shirt product, or it is a local beer, people tend to provide more consideration in the way that they feel about it. Mainly because an attack on that local product is an attack on them. They will also feel that the more local something is, the more compelled they will try to support it. Generally, people detest corporatism when it comes to products. They may shop at franchises or mass built stores, but if they can actually purchase something local, they will do so even if the price is higher a similar product available to them that is manufactured across the country. There is a nobility in localism which matters.

What sells with local does not sell with national. The idea that the public is pushing a product made by one of its owner. There is a power there. It allows them skin in the game, an ownership of being ahead of the curve compared to others. And to have something unique to themselves, rather than something everyone has access to. This is as tribal as it gets. Territorialism matters and it reflects the overall culture. Consider that this is helping the customer feel good, knowing that the money goes back into their community. And the seller is someone from their community, someone who is a neighbor, friend or associate. Not only of the buyer, but of people the buyer knows. This is a peer-angled sale as much as it is a straight-sale. Plus, if something goes wrong, there is a belief that a local person will attempt to correct the issue, especially a service, compared to a national brand.

The larger something gets, the less overall personal it feels. Mainly because it grows in mass, and there is a belief that the largess has made it forget about the little people who initially supported it. This is why people like to chat up a person that they think is the owner. It makes it more personal, but also provides the buyer with insight into how the product is made or sold. That matters for the overall basis of understanding and engaging story, which is a component of how word of mouth spreads, and how sales are driven. Story conquers all. Because it helps drive the conversation, between seller to buyer, but then buyer to potential buyer, about what the product is all about. This breaks down the larger something becomes. Because the story gets muddied and muddled. And after a while, people are unsure what they support about a massive product that they can no longer relate to.

The issue is that most local business fall into the mega marketing trap. That idea that they have to be bigger than themselves. Unless you have an investor cap for multiple stores, it is important to ensure that you are perceived as a local business. There is a difference between local and small. Never allow yourself to be perceived as small. This is one of the issues with the term "small business" – it suggests that you aren't big enough to handle a large load of business. Completely the opposite of how you want to be perceived. You can handle a lot of orders, but you are local business to the community. That is how the perception of your consumer reality needs to be.

Most of the small business you see is done as a side-gig hobby. Because people refuse to sustain themselves on the idea of generating enough profits for that small business to thrive into a larger local business. They are held back on the idea of owning a community, thinking that they have to own a region before they are worthy of being shown as a larger business. This is wrong-headed. The regional marketing plan is for investors. For the long-term thought process of expansion. But you need to be local in order for people to buy-in as a consumer, until you reach a certain status where you can handle the community not directly supporting you.

HIRE A BOOKKEEPER

The stupidest thing that anyone with a payroll can do is not include hiring a bookkeeper to manage it. Payroll may work the way it should, but a bookkeeper eliminates any of the doubts that get you in trouble later. Both state audit systems and the Internal Revenue Service are more than eager to jump on anyone who doesn't have a standardized bookkeeper. Whether that's an in-house person or someone who does bookkeeping professionally, it matters who sets up your accounts, and whether they can deliver a fair P&L to you. A lot of people think that they can get away with a good P&L, they tend to just do things themselves, what's the difference? And then, they get hit with an audit, or question about their finances, which sends most of their world crumbling, actively searching for receipts and excuses as to why they do not know their numbers. Most investors won't deal with someone who doesn't have a P&L for a reason. It's just sloppy business.

If you are operating a small business out of your house, where you are consulting or just collecting checks and spending out of one bank account, then you likely don't need a bookkeeper. You will need an accountant at the end of the year who will handle your return, mainly to discover deductions such as office and mileage write-offs, but the majority of the issues can be handled by you personally. The majority of royalty accounts are handled this way. There are only dollars coming in, that have to be taxed, instead of thousands of receipts, both income and expense, that have to be tracked. And when it comes to payroll, that's when you automatically have to hire a bookkeeper.

A bookkeeper keeps you involved, but they also pay ahead of time on state and federal taxation. They help you in your blind spots, as well as forecast where you are with your P&L. This is going to matter every month that you are in business. And a bookkeeper charges their hourly rate, but should also be able to cut it apart between several LLCs, if you are operating in that manner. All of this is to keep you from hurting your own business, or creating more expense, simply by trying to do it yourself.

Beyond anything else, you need to establish a relationship with a bookkeeper. You want to work together with someone who has all of your financial interests? Get to know them. It's important. Especially because you find out how much you can actually trust them. It goes beyond merely securing what you think is a good rate. Besides, sometimes, those bookkeepers who cost more aren't worth more. Mainly because they have fewer clients and don't really take the job as seriously as they should. Responsiveness, especially through email or text on general questions, is a good indicator on whether or not a specific bookkeeper is right for you.

The thing about a bookkeeper, much like an accountant, is that you have to be financially naked in front of them. There is no place to hide. If you aren't willing to showcase everything that you've done in your business, you shouldn't be in business, nor should you have a bookkeeper. When I'm starting a new venture personally, I look down the road and ask myself if I need a bookkeeper on this business project. And if I ever see myself needing a bookkeeper for a specific project, then I hire them from the start, because it will keep my entire financial outlook in that business on the straight and narrow from the beginning. What you spend now is what you end up saving later.

Your bookkeeper can be a swell person, but they are not your friend or buddy. They are the person who can show you what money you are hemorrhaging and what money you are generating via net profit margin. They can also break down several categories of expense, allowing you to see what you are spending way too much on. A good P&L does this, and a lot of people avoid having a P&L because of it. They just don't want to know what they are spending money on, except when their debits exceed their credits, then they want to know why no one told them what was happening. A bookkeeper can act like a problem solver in this regard. They can flag a lot of payments ahead of time to ensure that your bank account isn't being sliced apart via death by a thousand paper cuts (small issues that end up creating a lot of expense when totaled out).

A bookkeeper also is a way to enact cost controls. Especially when it comes to labor ratios. It is a good set of fresh eyes on a problem that can grow out of control. When a bookkeeper looks at a situation, they can evaluate whether the hours used by the employees earning the most actually generate a higher amount of revenue for the business. That may seem a bit complex, but its accurate and important. Just as there is revenue per square foot, there is also revenue per employee hour. Let's say that your business brings in $1,400 on a specific day, but you have three employees earning $23 each for the six hours that it takes to generate that amount of money.

That's $414 spent, plus all of the wonderful taxes, so let's round it up to $650, in order to generate $1,400 gross. So that's really $750 that you brought home, except now you have to account for the other overheads such as utilities, lease, marketing, etc. In essence, you may have been better off having one employee at $27 and two employees making minimum at $13.69 (Washington State's highest minimum wage in the union price in 2017 - it keeps going up to 2024's $16.28 and rising annually to $16.66 in 2025). I do think the $16.66 minimum wage in 2025, a 2.35% increase over 2024, is rather insidious and humorous if you read between the lines. It's almost a small business apocalypse waging. That might actually get you to closer to where you want to be. As mentioned in previous chapters, labor ratios are sometimes your best way of reducing overall costs and increasing net profit margin. And this is why a great bookkeeper will help with forecasting and cost controls, to prevent you from losing your shirt by ensuring that you know in advance what is being spent, etc.

KNOW YOUR LANDLORD

Your landlord could be your best friend or your worst enemy. Always get everything in spelled out in a lease and have it reviewed by a lawyer. It doesn't matter whether you've known the person forever or not, things can change. Especially if there's a person in their ear who doesn't care about you or what you think. You may be a tenant, but as with anything, it's all what's either spelled out in the contract or not included at all. Your lease matters to you in order to hold the landlord accountable.

Beyond that, it is important to understand what the landlord is also going through at multiple times. People view a landlord as an easy proposition; but he or she is in business as anything else. As property taxation always hit landlords, those costs, including those of utilities and repair, tend to burden the landlord as much as the small businesses that he or she rents to. Your involvement as a small business owner is as much of a symbiotic relationship in protecting their asset (i.e. the building structure itself) as it is your business inside of the building. One cannot exist without the other, especially if you are witnessing vagrants or ne'er-do-wells around the building.

You should also be aware if the building is handled by a management company. This arm's length approach works for some landlords, but also keeps some repairs from occurring. Now with another hand in the cookie jar, there is less money from each rental unit to pay for things, including repairs. The landlord is also a person on an island. Even if the business that you have fails, the landlord must still exist in the same spot. Moving a building is not possible and the municipalities know that, which is why they are always ready with more commercial property taxes, waiting to pay for wonderful things that didn't exist the day prior.

I would recommend finding others who have leased from the landlord prior to signing anything or even engaging in the lease process yourself. Why get involved if you find out that the landlord is aloof or worse, a kook? This occurs more often than you think. There are landlords who have family money and are absent-minded when it comes to repairs or structural soundness. They may also allow their public bathrooms to sport leaky toilets, rusty pipes or be uncleaned because the costs associated are not something that they want to take on. Remember, everything in your lease is all that you will get from your lease. And even then, it may be too much to ask that your landlord live up to the lease. Depends on who you are dealing with. Reference check your landlord prior to even the first conversation with them about the space.

Is your landlord is mentally prepared to accumulate someone else's business, equipment and operation? They may do so if you fail to product rent. Then the locks get changed, and they sell your business for scrap, while putting a lien on your private home, etc. for the unpaid rent plus other fees. So, this is where I almost talk you out of getting a commercial space altogether. Do you actually need that much space? How small can you make the business, or at least the storage of the business, prior to generating a profit? If you have a garage at your house or even a small storage space, you have a business. If you are doing a photography studio, why can't you use space in a spare bedroom? When you are generating profit, it is to your detriment to lease out space that will go unused or won't help attract customers. Certain businesses need commercial space, and certain spaces do not. The more of your overhead that you control, the better it is for the long-term sustainability of the business.

Every human gets into a weird mode of the temporary impressing of others. Notice the "validation" pictures of people on social media, showing which car they purchased, which spouse they married or what ring they chose from the engagement. While it is nice to be happy for people's success, some of it is less about you seeing it, as much as it you "validating" their decision with a comment or a like. And all of that fades. With any of these things, you are building up new overhead on your life, much like your small business. Getting a new truck when a used one will do is simply flashing success while not sharing that you've doubled your car loan payment. Leasing a commercial space, when you do not need one, is no different. Your friends will venture through the commercial space once or twice, tell you how impressed they are, then return to their lives. So, you basically signed a 5-year commercial lease so you could brag to your friends, rather than ensure that the business could properly use the space efficiently, to generate the most profit. Not very smart, in my opinion.

I mentioned the wine snob previously. He and I had originally formed the wine sales company. We did so out of an office suite for a $475 month payment for a 475-square-foot office. Despite generating some profit, the wine snob wanted a store front. He needed a store front desperately. And so we separated on good terms. He bought into a store front, and did okay, but the issue was now he had to cover those units of time with his presence. Or hire someone else to. This is what commercial retail real estate does. It forces you to be available when the customer decides to show up, rather than appointment setting with the customer to ensure that they have a specific window of time that they are guaranteeing to show up. The wine snob's overhead increased because of his perception of how much retail time service his customer needed, rather than the reality that if you have great wine, customers will set appointments and show up at your office door for it.

So, now I have done my good deed and attempted to get you to think about whether you need a commercial space or not. If anything, it got your mind working a little. I cannot make decisions for you, but as we get into commercial leases and structures, it is important to separate the signal from the noise. It is great to impress your friends with a commercial space, but if it doesn't work for the business operation, it doesn't work for you. Be prepared for the math of overhead. There's a cost to everything.

YOUR LEASE

There lies a specific turning point in any business. You have to determine whether this is a brick & mortar operation, or a home office operation. It cannot be both. Brick & mortar operation is what a McDonald's looks like. Something to where you are build to suit leasing opportunities or buying the land outright, but still in a commercialized zone. Your customers come to you, park their cars, and visit your operation in order for you to turn a buck. The alternative is a home office situation where you are basically making phone calls, taking orders, doing consulting work, collecting royalties, but rarely if ever,

greeting customers where you live. That is what a home office is for –
likely in your home, writing off a spare bedroom as a piece of square
footage on your taxes.

Your P&L rides on you knowing where you are going to plant your
ability to produce commerce, and whether you can delineate how that
commerce exchange happens. Way too often, entrepreneurs see that
they need a big storefront in a physical location for something that
can be done at a home office. They need to have a place where clients
can meet them, be impressed because there is an assistant out front,
and see that the business is big time. This is an overhead expense that
often can be eliminated. Not only in square footage, but also in idle
labor hours by an assistant who may be unneeded. If you can figure
out a scheduling app, meet at a coffee shop, or even lease a meeting
room at a building for two hours, you don't need all of the unnecessary
overhead of a brick & mortar storefront.

Decide what it is that you are doing. Are you shaking hands with
customers to gain agreements while establishing guidelines of
service? That's a home office trade. Are you having a mass amount
of customers arrive into your location, where they select something
off of the shelf, walk up to a counter, then purchase it and potentially
stick around a while? That is a brick & mortar storefront. These things
have to be deciphered as part of your overall business plan. Mainly
because if you don't need it, then you shouldn't lease it. This type
of overhead is not only costly, but also dangerous to the long-term
ability of your startup's survival. Yet, people choose to do it to impress
others. Much like purchasing a six-bedroom McMansion when you
are a young couple with limited incomes. It sounds great to host three
family parties a year in that type of house, but the rest of the space is
likely an albatross of monthly mortgage payments at 300% higher than
you would pay for a normal, two-bedroom duplex. Because you are

not looking at the underlying costs of upkeep which soar beyond the expectation, as you are no longer a renter, but a home owner.

Brick & Mortar comes with a lot of issues that you will not have at the home office. If you want to attract people to your place, it has to be nice. It also has to be in a great location, where you take foot traffic, parking and other elements into account. You also had to ensure that it is up to code. That's the rub, the amount of city code, permits and underlying lease obligations that you haven't been thinking about until after you've signed on that dotted line. The second you sign the lease, you are beholden to a contract which may or may not specify what obligations you, as well as the landlord, have to each other. As well as to the city itself, which seems more than willing to let you sit in a limbo while it hits you with zoning and permits and fees, because that's how a municipality makes its money. Any municipality can resemble the old school mobsters, except that they don't whack you once, but over and over again, with yet another fee to pay for their cost overruns later. They love fees, such as impact fees, which are assessed in ways to ensure that businesses keep paying, over and over again, for the same services on an annual basis.

The home office is not a good place for foot traffic, but if you can sell it over the internet using your garage as the initial warehouse, or if you can perform consulting services while meeting at coffee shops, you eliminate insurance, lease agreements with commercial landlords, and other specific expenses. Brick & mortar is where you cook a burger or serve a drink. A lot of the folks working from home these days, post-COVID-19, are doing so based off the idea that it eliminates a lot of overhead for their employers, who no longer are requiring office space overhead. Insurers, real estate agents and other business sales staff focused on customer (B2C) or business to business (B2B) are finding out that their home internet, printer and office setup will eliminate more overhead costs to their employer which increasing their employee costs overall.

A Brick & Mortar operation means that you are tying yourself to a city. That means its politics, its viewpoint on commerce, its overall strategy and whether or not it will create new barriers to hinder your ability to drive foot traffic, thus revenue, to your place of business. Seattle in 2020 created a payroll tax which was directed specifically at larger companies such as Amazon, but it effected smaller businesses such as restaurants and shops, as Amazon started to move those 10,000 jobs out of the Seattle downtown core, instead into neighboring Bellevue. This was a city council strategy that backfired, and instead, caused an effect on smaller businesses throughout the downtown area and of greater Seattle in general. Entrepreneurship means being aware of new rules, viewpoints and laws that are put on the books or being proposed by city officials, and how that will affect your bottom line to operate.

Cities do not have a real understanding of commerce. A lot of municipalities will buy into the idea that they do, but the majority of city officials are part-time, and are very small business owners or tend to be employees of state government. They are in it with good intentions, but rarely have the small business mentality of utilizing a start-up venture, nor know truly what it takes to survive and thrive. Thus, they are usually the first types of politicians who propose B&O taxations, misunderstanding who pays B&O. The small business operation affected by B&O does not pay that tax, their customers do, thus the tax burden is pushed off onto area citizens, who end up paying more for the same service.

Nor do cities really know how to market. Especially downtown districts. For over six decades, the common thread of city marketing is how to "revive" a downtown district. They usually overspend on things like minor league baseball teams but do less for individual small businesses such as lowering taxation, creating new avenues of collective promotional support, etc. City management is practically useless in a marketing sense, much like an economic development council. They essentially look at the numbers after the fact, then determine whether it was a success or failure. Cities are also slower to move because of open governance laws and oversight by citizen-elected councils who are typically part-time, and sometimes have competing interests when it comes to abatements and zoning restrictions.

When you decide to go Brick & Mortar, you are tying yourself to a city. All of its positive and negative issues. You don't get to choose whether it's a good thing after the fact, until your commercial lease is done. Which means that if the city that you put your business into has a massive homeless, drug or otherwise vagrant issue, well, you are now locked in. Just because the lease is cheap doesn't mean that you now don't have to deal with the fallout, such as parking issues for your customers. The more car traffic you get into that area, the more likely street parking has meters installed to charge those customers. All of this comes into the complexity of having a Brick & Mortar location.

I've had both Brick & Mortar and home office operations. It depends what you are selling and whether you can get away with not carrying a commercial overhead lease. Home office operations are a good plan if you don't require a lot of customer foot traffic to your actual location. Perhaps you have a website and can provide distribution, or you perform consulting services over Zoom or the phone. All of these options allow for a home office operation where you can move it to the area of your choice. It also means that if a city environment goes wrong with its politics, say, defunding the police, well, you can move to a climate where they fund the police, thus the crime levels will be lower, etc. Politics plays a lot into where a small business thrives.

The whole point of comparing Brick & Mortar with Home office operation is asking, whether or not it is worth it to have a physical location for customers to go to. The overhead issue can be a top-heavy concern for startups, and if they can avoid having a physical location, it is recommended in the early stages in order to survive and thrive. Home office operations also don't have several of the limitations that a Brick & Mortar has, minus the inability to host a lot of customer foot traffic. No home owner association (HOA) wants to see a line of cars parked daily along the neighborhood street, coming to one house which serves as a business. That's why there remains zoning for residential houses compared to mixed-use houses which can offer that type of physical foot traffic commerce.

Home office operations are a bit different. They are out of your house, you have a certain amount of square footage space that you can write-off to the IRS in your Schedule C form, and you kinda control the environment. It is more of an "eat what you kill" ecosystem because unlike Brick & Mortar, you cannot count on anyone stopping by randomly, purchasing your product, and making your monthly revenue goal. You have to really earn it, usually by phone, Zoom or email. And quite possibly a combination of all three. You also do not have to sign a personal guarantee against your retirement or your house when you have a home office operation. When you have a commercial lease, they get paid regardless of whether you make money.

So, now that we've looked at Brick & Mortar or Home office operation, it comes down to understanding why you feel you need such a large overhead cost at all. What is it that you are attempting to do? There are several ways to generate money, and several methods in order to make money without accumulating massive amounts of overhead. People unfortunately see the end result of their vision, not the early stages which may not have the finished building in mind. Having the idea that you start from a massive high rise means that you are forsaken to the potential cost to build something, despite having less than credible funds to support it. You need to start small, think light, and grow.

Small commercial retail spaces often suffer from a lack of vision by their start-up creators. Give me 500-600 square feet at a $900 all-inclusive lease (meaning electricity and water are wrapped into the rental lease price) for a five year lease plus five year option, and you've got a safe business moving forward. Whatever you do, the ability to clear $1500 a month shouldn't be difficult. That includes insurance and any other overhead that you might have. Sure, you may have to work the retail location yourself, in order to ensure that your labor costs aren't out of control, but even staffing one person with 500-600 square feet isn't difficult to use as an entire service area.

There are some sticking points to any commercial space, especially when they are newly developed parcels of land or re-developed buildings. Frankly, the developer falls in love with a price because it is a portion of what he/she paid for the building. So they stick with that price for 6-to-12 months, until they discover the market conditions aren't relative to their initial asking price. The other issue is the lending unit, which was sold on providing commercial loan services based on certain market conditions and commercial leased space options. So even if the developer or landlord wants to charge a lower price, they are unable to based on the lending company's insistence on what to charge for the space. This happens a lot with newly developed or re-developed buildings, where there are several commercial street level and multiple floor spaces available, but at above-market asking price, and either the landlord or the lender are unwilling to allow those spaces to be leased for less.

Another barrier to building up a start-up is a negative mindset. This is something that can be overcome only if you personally decide to change it. I've encountered several people who are risk-adverse. Meaning that they are so certain that a start-up needs to gain a 4-to-1 automatic return that they are hesitant or resistant to actually moving forward, because of the uncertainty of actually gaining a profit. A loss, even a small one, scares them away entirely. A lot of great ideas for start-ups remain that; ideas. Specifically because those who have the ideas, even if they have the funds, refuse to commit the time, energy and passion required to move forward. Worse yet, they focus on assumptions; they assume what the lease will cost, what the issues will be, or how customers will engage. They waste the time of others, hashing out ideas about what they want to have as a start-up, only to freeze at their own 45-yard-line (i.e. 55 percent of the way to moving forward) because of the fear of risk. Everything in life is risk, including a smaller commercial retail space. Mainly because you are making a five-year commitment, not even a one-year commitment with a residential. It scares people off entirely from projects that they want to be a part of, because making money isn't cheap, fair or certain. There is no risk without reward, even when renting smaller commercial spaces.

The thing is, these types of spaces often get glossed over by potential commercial retail start-ups. They see the small space and instantly think about growing larger. You can always grow larger and beyond a small space. It's the potential of being consumed by overhead costs, especially with labor and the need to fill a specific amount of square footage, which will make the difference between a business surviving or thriving. While I am using the example of physical square footage being small, it is also to suggest that you may not need a physical location, or overhead lease, in order to grow a startup from scratch. And I have a couple of examples which illustrate the lack of need for commercial space, while building a startup business.

Chair renting for hair stylists and tattoo artists is a great way to incorporate the idea of what business the person carrying the lease is in. They are effectively less of a hair stylist than a landlord themselves, charging for the ability to handle all of the overhead costs, creating an all-inclusive system for hair stylists and tattoo artists (i.e. sub-leasers) to work in. It is interesting that, despite this, these sub-leasers rarely do the little things. A way for sub-leasers to generate more income is to book out months in advance based on chair hours available, and increase the amount of volume.

This is where dynamic pricing comes in. The more that people want something, the higher the price goes. Meaning that the sub-leasers should be increasing their prices by 17-percent after 80-percent of their bookable hours are taken. So, if it's $30 for a haircut, after 80 percent of the bookings are taken, then it becomes $35.10. Which may not seem like a lot, except that with 20 percent more bookings in place, that creates a volume of $100 per full booking extra. That could be a day, or a week, and doesn't include tips. I'm also a big believer in the sub-leaser controlling the tip situation themselves. Too often, tips start at the lowest amount of 10 percent, which makes it way too easy for customers to get off of the hook. At my cider bar location, we started tips at 25 percent, 42 percent, 67 percent and 100 percent. Mainly because it motivated customers to do math, thus helping the servers generate money income. And none of the servers complained about receiving 100 percent tips either.

This is where Triple Net comes into play. You will hear this term a lot in commercial leasing. It means that you as the lessee, are on the hook for all real estate taxes, building insurance, and maintenance (the three nets) of the property. In addition, you are required to also pay normalized fees such as rent, utilities, etc. Triple Net is essentially a way for the building owner to avoid several taxation types from various businesses that rent from them. And they pass on the cost to you, the lessee. Especially maintenance, which is a crooked way of saying that if the ceiling caves in, you are required to fix it under a Triple Net lease, even if the maintenance issue was created prior to your arrival.

Everything is about a mindset. A karate or mixed martial arts training does not necessarily need to start out in a 4,000 square foot gym. If weather permits, why not book for students to train outside? Do it in a public park, either by booked field at $25 an hour or by just showing up to the space on a Tuesday. It will depend again on the hour and the weather, but it can be done low-level, until you build up a certain amount of students who pay per session hour. Let's say you have 10 students at $65 per session hour, for 5 hours per week and 4 weeks per month. That's $3,250 per week and $13,000 per month. Then, you can afford the overhead of a space. Why charge so much per session hour? Because it is actually low enough to ensure that if you have a certain amount of students within the week or month fill out the hours, you will cover and make money on costs.

Once you gain a space, at likely $2,500 - $5,000 a month, you have to factor in what you are going to do with the remaining hours of the space once your sessions are done. Notice that under the scenario, you are only using five hours per week, and twenty hours per month. There are 168 hours in a seven day week. There are 744 hours in a 31 day month. And if you are using only 20 hours total of that month in order to train people, it is time to convenience what can be done within that space during the idle hours. What if you sublet the space to other teachers to have their own training, charging them at $10 per student? Or installed exercise gym equipment to have the space utilized at a rate of $200 per hour? Now your $13,000 revenue stream has a $148,800 secondary stream coupled with it. Math is fun when you start to calculate what is gained by subletting or utilizing space in secondary functions. It also points out that your love of the original product may not be in as high of demand as your secondary product.

So, here is that word of warning. Don't fall in love with a specific prospective space. Look at a lot of spaces. Know what you want, but realize that once you become enamored with a space, it's the wrong move. Too many factors play into a space, and not just the surroundings of whatever foot traffic goes on around it. You also have landlords, buildings that may crumble, and the city to factor in. Make sure that you go in on the right space for you, but also weigh all of the other factors that may not be present from the beginning. This is a long-term marriage with commercial leasing. You don't get month-to-month or even a 12-month deal like you do in residential leasing unless the landlord is shady, old or someone who might jack up the rent when your foot traffic catches their attention.

This is where the fun really begins: What if you sell your business? In a way, your lease will dictate how much authority your landlord has in who you sell to. If the lease says that your landlord has final ownership approval, it may stop you from selling to the person with the most money. This is one of the factors that you have to get cleared with the landlord prior, when you first decide to sign a lease. Simply put, anyone can walk up, hand you a check for 25% higher than your asking price, but still not be cleared by the landlord to be put on the lease. The landlord may force your hand, require you to remain on the lease as a guarantor, in case the new owner of your business decides to run in the middle of the night.

You should also ensure that any tenant improvements credited to the lease also have contractors who have their own commercial insurance. Don't venture under the table only to find out that they screw up on the plumbing, now you've caused the entire building to have foundation or sink issues. Yes, you probably have the skills to trench a commercial floor for a water pipe or sewage installation for that required bathroom to your coffee shop. However, you should really know the cost if you screw up. Sometimes, hiring a private contractor with their own insurance saves you a lot more in the long-term. You can also ensure by contract that the private contractor will repair any issues that they caused, going through the extra effort so you don't have to.

THE RABBIT HOLE OF COMMERCIAL INSURANCE

If you ever want to know the bane of every entrepreneur's existence, it usually hinges on the details of commercial insurance. A necessary evil in a world where everyone is sue-happy, commercial insurance also robs the entrepreneur of time and paperwork above all else. And some capital. Again, commercial insurance is necessary, I would never recommend avoiding it. However, it is a pain in the tailpipe to get, and even when you have it, you don't really have it the way you think you do.

Businesses during the COVID-19 shutdowns thought that they had commercial insurance protections regarding "gaps" in operation. Then the language seemingly was changed, suddenly broken windows by rioters during the 2020 summer were declared an "act of war" by insurers, and retail businesses had to fund their window replacements themselves. Commercial insurance has a team of lawyers at every brokerage, ready to fight every claim. They are the pit bull attack dog that you need when you get false "slip fall" claims from shady customers. However, those pit bull attack dogs will turn on you the second your business files a claim. All you need to know is that you pay the premium up-front for the year, unlike residential insurance, and you never act as if there's an opportunity to access a claim for your business, even if you have a true need to do so.

Commercial insurance is not simply calling up your agent and discovering what you can do. Well, then again, yes it is. Because a lot of commercial insurance is an extension of what your insurance can and cannot do. Sometimes, you can even attach it to your home owners insurance. All depending again, on what you want to do. When you form an LLC however, there are some breakages when it comes to insurance lines. You are effectively creating a separate entity (a corporation), and thereby also creating a separation between your public and corporate life.

When you delve into it, some of this is for your own benefit. You don't want your personal insurance rating decided by an LLC, which you may have to at some point bankrupt. Whether you think that will happen or not, the chances of bankrupt assumption may be too risky to tie your own home to it. Then again, there's also the issue of alcohol, which a lot of commercial insurers won't do. This is part of that overall evaluation of what you are doing, as well as what your commercial insurer can cover. And whether or not you want the same agent covering your home compared to your business. Sometimes, it is best to keep both far apart from each other.

Commercial insurance is not the same as what you get for your home, auto or life. It is an insurance against property liability claims, when someone steps foot in your business and might actually hit you with a claim. Yes, this will occur more than you think. Whenever you put up a shingle that says you are in business, you are going to encounter people whose entire reasoning for entering your business is to file a claim against your business, mainly because that is the business that you are in. You may think that you can get away with not carrying insurance, some commercial property owners who lease to you won't check, but it would be foolhardy to do so. Especially when someone claims a slip-fall in your business, then attempts to sue you for thousands in recovery.

The beauty of commercial insurance is that you also get an agent to walk you through the process of what you should be looking at in terms of coverage. Especially if you are leasing retail or restaurant space. All of the variables that you should not attempt to skim on. This isn't like your auto insurance, where you don't have to carry every premium. Keep in mind, some of the insurance is related not only to customer claims, but to the claims of property as well as protection against an employee being harmed in the workplace. This matters as well, as employees often may cause their own accidents through some fault of their own, and file a claim against your business. This includes issues of sexual harassment. Plus, if someone attempts to rob your business, it is smart to inform all employees to just give the money to the robber, that you are insured, rather than have the employee attempt to impede the thief and cause potential harm to themselves or customers in the process.

The thing that always stops new business owners from commercial insurance is the up-front cost of the premium. Commercial insurance isn't like an auto insurance premium, where it is spread out across the entire lifetime of the 6-to-12 month coverage cycle. Instead, commercial insurance is money upfront. The entire premium paid out for the 12-months. It can be difficult to shell out that type of premium at once, when you haven't brought in a dime. However, it is sometimes necessary in the overall aspect of the coverage. Some commercial insurers will work with clients that they trust, and create a spread out payment plan, with interest, in order to make the payments easier on the business overall.

Everything in commercial insurance is about paying those premiums as well as checking in with your insurer about coverage and claims. Never for a moment leave anything to chance. If you are doing anything at all that may change that claim, check with your commercial insurance agent. This is often how folks lose out on claims or end up going bankrupt when in business, because they didn't check with their insurer before extending themselves beyond what their coverage allows. If you aren't supposed to transport business supplies in your personal vehicle, but do so anyway, you are opening yourself to liability issues if you get in an accident. These are the tightrope methods of insurance issues that all commercial insurers as well as their clients, have to walk when discussing what coverage may disallow. It is smart to have a good relationship with your commercial insurance from the start.

In Washington state, where the 1762 logic of Jean-Jacques Rousseau's Social Contract does not apply, anything goes as long as you do it as a criminal. If you do it as a business, you will be fined and busted for arrest. However, as a criminal, you will not be cited and the matter will be shrugged off. In 2020, the state passed a piece of "police pursuit" legislation which did not allow police to chase criminals in stolen cars. By 2023, the amount of retail robberies skyrocketed with criminals first stealing cars, then driving the cars into the retail's front window, then escaping in another stolen car where the police could not pursue them. Commercial insurance premiums for retail businesses in Washington state has also skyrocketed, since the amount of claims have been moving up in connection with the blatant criminal acts.

Every LLC likely needs its own insurance premium. But that depends on what you are trying to do. If you are a consultant working with banks or university campuses, they will require certain insurance coverages before working with you. It's a part of mitigating their own liability risks with their own insurers should your consulting recommendations be viewed as causing harm to someone who files a claim against you. As with everything, this comes down to the horrific nature of customer-based claims which are filed in a frivolous nature. It is its own industry for grifters who raise the cost to everyone else, because they file claims of zero merit, hoping to seek out the business without insurance protection or an insurer who would rather pay them off instead of fighting the claim. It is important that you actively look at your commercial insurance options, to ensure that you are working with an insurer who will fight for you and provide the coverage of protection that you require.

This comes into the realm of specialty insurance such as liquor liability. Every bar or restaurant or any entity involved in alcohol needs to have some variant of liquor liability insurance. This is one of the hottest areas of claims against a business, especially with the driving under the influence and minor in possession laws across the country. Liquor liability insurance is to protect against someone being harmed by another person who is under the influence of alcohol, who claims that they were over-served in your establishment. Everything is a crap running downhill scenario where, once personal injury lawyers get involved, is about trying to find a business deemed responsible for the claim so that they can be paid out as a result. If generally, there is an industry of people filing frivolous claims against businesses, so too is there an industry of lawyers willing to support those frivolous claims which clog the American legal system as well.

The majority of the commercial insurance, once it becomes too big, goes out to the big black hole of brokerage. This is where it takes forever and a day to learn whether or not your new start-up business will earn coverage. These brokerage groups are massive. They also talk to each other, so it makes it more difficult to shop around for better insurance premiums. Once it goes to brokerage, everything changes as you are in a wait and see mode of doing business overall. It is smart to work with a commercial insurance agent from the conceptual base of the business idea, before you've even done much of anything, and work out from there. Use prospective business addresses on potential retail establishment locations to help see what the premiums are, then go from there.

Commercial insurance is about the long-game approach. Every LLC doesn't need commercial insurance. But those that want to succeed should have it. If you are over-insured past a certain point, you are merely paying a lot of premiums for a lack of gain. But when you are dealing with the public, everything changes. Especially on who or what can be claimed against your business, and against whatever assets that you have.

THE 48 MONTH VOW

Uh, oh... What if that "yes, but..." guy on your shoulder was right? What if this is too much. Literally, so much risk that even the risk-taker on your other shoulder is no longer taking your calls? It is very humbling to jump into all of the different math components, knowing that the risk is there. Look, everyone who does anything to generate money independently of someone else's company is taking a risk. This book may not sell all 59 paperback copies that it would need to, over its lifetime, in order to cover the $379 expense through a $5.89 royalty recoupment. This is why you have to factor in the gamble that where there is risk, there can be failure or reward. Once you humble yourself to that reality, you will be better for it.

So, now comes the hard part. A topic that everyone hates. If you truly want your start-up small business to survive. You cannot withdraw money from it. Forty-eight months. Four years. This is a commitment to yourself as an entrepreneur. This is a vow. That you will attempt to survive by not withdrawing from the business. Instead, you will put as much as you can back into the business. Think about that commitment. Think about what it means to your staff, to you, to commit every possible dollar back into the business. The reason that business owners do not attempt this is often they are getting into entrepreneurship for the wrong reasons. They want to essentially quit working. They've cashed in their retirement, and are basically living off of the funding model they've created. So, every dollar goes back into paying themselves for making the investment in the first place.

And that's why they often do not have the funding to expand. Or survive in a lot of cases. This type of action is a race to the bottom. It ignores the idea that you might be part of the market trend, upward, then downward. It ignores that world, regional and local events may cause your business to collapse. Such as COVID-19, or even a large snowstorm which stops your entire customer base from getting to you. All of this awaits you as a business owner. And when you do not have a contingency, when you do not re-invest into your own company, it is hard to survive. Especially at the small business level.

We have a tendency now to only focus on tech start-ups. Those who are seemingly awash in cash from angel fundraising rounds. But notice that in 2022 and 2023, tech companies started to be severely questioned by their cash burn rates. Were they actually generating customers, or merely burning as much capital as possible while enjoying a "tech bro" lifestyle of partying in Silicon Valley? Suddenly, those groups started to do layoffs and cutbacks. The laptop generation who spent all of their free time criticizing hard labor jobs, telling them to "learn to code" during layoffs, were laid-off themselves with little sympathy. Amazing how those who show a lack of empathy for others tend to earn the same reaction when it is their turn at the Guillotine.

Any entrepreneur who is focused on scaling up needs to ensure that they are at the smallest space possible to begin. To not spend more than they should during that first 48 months (sometimes a bit longer), until you have a handle on your customer base and can drive sales. Often, outside suggestions will see your business as expandible. They will want you every 5 miles away from your original location. This means more overhead, employees, more things to manage. And unless you have the capital along with the sustainable customer base to support it, you should ignore those calls. Expanding for expansion sake does not but create overhead, problems and more five-year commercial leases. You have got to ensure that when you start a business, you understand not only the business but the on-boarding structure surrounding it.

The first 48 months is a commitment to yourself to be diligent. That you've done not only your homework prior, but that you are ready to put forward the effort required to make this company work for the long-term. Commitment is a funny thing these days. For better or worse doesn't necessarily mean what it used to mean. Now, you're a Tik-Tok version away from a divorce party. People see these former structures of combining goals and commitment as something to shrug off. The same as a business. They do not want to fully work the business once it gets boring, or mundane. I would question why they decided to take the plunge in the first place, but that would mean accountability, and that's generally not what you are going to get as a response.

So, let's say you've made a bit of money beyond all of the taxes, and cost per unit, and you are sitting on a healthy net profit margin. What do you do with it? You reinvest it into the business. All of it. For the first year, do not assume that you can make money off of your venture and use it for non-business functions. You need to reinvest it. Grow your business by improving your systems, expanding your product lines, and knowing the business of your business. This is the hardest piece of education for any entrepreneur. They want to live the way they see idiots on television do, lying on a pile of bills, driving a bunch of cars, etc. If you truly want to grow your brand, you need to reinvest it.

That means learning more about your store. Daily. Figuring out nuances which only come to light after you have met and engaged with customers. You have to work the store. Even if it's not physical, even if it's only online. When you simply allow cookie cutter solutions, you get cookie cutter results. You should be engaged, trying your best to ensure that every nuance of the store comes to light.

REVENUE PER SQUARE FOOT

Most businesses should adhere to a revenue per square foot calculation. It is a simple, second grade math education basic formula. How much income can you take in, monthly, per square foot of your business? If you don't know the answer, you should discover it. A grocery store at 25,000 square feet with a $45,000 monthly revenue plus $50,000 in monthly payroll, has a weight of $95,000 against it without considering other overhead such as lights, sewer garbage, and inventory. With a revolving inventory of $500,000 or more possible each week, this creates its own havoc within the revenue per square calculation. Let's assume that the 25,000 square foot grocery store, with a monthly overhead of $750,000 needs to figure out its revenue per square foot. That means that each square foot is already costing the grocery store $30, before it makes a dime of profit.

Once you dissect this further, in order to make a profit, the grocery store would have to generate $60 per each square foot in order to be solvent. Remember, you have to pay taxes, wage increases, shipping supply and inventory costs. You cannot simply divide the cost by the square footage and assume that break-even is actually break-even. Let's not forget all of the other fees associated as a part of the sunken costs, including transaction fees, marketing, and spoilage. You have to equate for all of these within your revenue per square foot model of business. Doubling your expectation against your need, it allows you to see every single point of how to generate revenue off of every piece of square footage that you have on average. You need to know how to squeeze as much revenue out of a space as possible in order to survive.

As mentioned in another chapter called Retail Ancillaries, knickknacks at the cash register of a convenience store matter. They take up very little space, are found at every cash register, and end up generating a high enough profit margin. Because the rest of the space inside of the grocery store needs to have some manageability of people walking around with a shopping cart in order to purchase things. But this doesn't simply have to stay at a grocery store level. Any operation worth its salt should be looking at as well as calculating out their revenue per square foot model. If there is a place that needs to have product there to purchase, such as a small gift shop in a giant family fun center, it requires you to know not only the original inventory cost, but also how to turn over that revenue enough to make the revenue per square foot model sustainable.

If you cannot bring home the revenue, then the entire effort is not worth it. This should be your mantra to follow as you make different attempts to cycle through products that can be purchased, then replaced with backroom inventory. Your goal is to have enough that people never actually run out of an item on the shelf, but that also feel like those items will be out of stock if they do not buy it today. This turns over the revenue. Other items include small vending machines or other products that help transform a space into a revenue generator beyond your original products that you sell. Sometimes, there is too much space for too little inventory. Consider that when you are walking that space for the first time, looking at what you are selling. If there is an empty void of space in the corner, figure out how to place something there that will yield you out the revenue return on investment that you are seeking and increases your revenue per square foot calculation.

A lot of business owners don't see the need for t-shirts or other knickknacks because that's not their style. But if the customer wants one, if the customer is willing to pay for one, then you should provide it. Especially if it means that you will yield out a larger revenue stream off of a low-cost item. Your revenue per square foot model is also a cost per square foot model. It shows you where the holes are in your system. It shows you what you are giving up, and what you should be fighting for.

YOUR EQUIPMENT

I am a hound for finding used commercial equipment from online auctions. In 2021, I sourced out an entire commercial kitchen sink worth about $1,800. I was able to purchase it for less than $200 cash. The only issue was that the sink was still screwed into the walls of the Seattle pizza joint where I, along with my friend, David, showed up to purchase. That is the other component of online auctions - you are required to do the heavy lifting to remove the purchased commercial equipment from the premises. It took David and I about 10 seconds to recognize why the Seattle pizza joint had closed and it was not due to COVID-19 shutdown restrictions. Aside from the black mold and slime, there were cockroaches everywhere. Literally, everywhere. David got sick to his stomach, questioned whether we should proceed, and together we ripped the three parts of the commercial kitchen sink out of the wall. Cockroaches went flying everywhere - some of them had little wings and buzzed us as we left the kitchen with the commercial sink.

We drove it back to a city warehouse space that I rented from. The City of Lacey had a warehouse that they had purchased for $1.6 million, then left empty, avoiding contractors who kept inquiring about leasing the space for $35,000 a month. In 48 months, the city would have earned back its entire purchase price. However, this is a municipality, and they had "visioned" for a new city museum on the site of the warehouse. In 2022, they toppled the building entirely and paved it as a parking lot, to the tune of $700,000. There's no museum on site.

But at the time of 2021, while the city was still resisting calls to lease, I had a rental agreement in place. $212 per month for about 150,000 square feet to store whatever I liked. Including a large cider van. And a bunch of commercial kitchen equipment. Including a three part commercial kitchen sink, which I cleaned up, and then sold on Facebook marketplace for $1,000 cash. Thus I generated an $800 profit off of being willing to clean up some commercial pieces of metal with industrial chemicals, selling them to someone else who didn't know where I got it from. All they knew was that they wanted the commercial kitchen sink, so it was worth it to them. Minus the black slime or cockroaches, which weren't a part of the deal nor mentioned to the buyers. Therein lies the issue of commercial kitchen equipment. No one truly knows what it's worth. But used is just as good as new.

A great big black hole of any business is in the equipment that it purchases. When starting out, small business owners often try to rely on consumer equipment, even for printers or computers, only to discover that the heavy toll of business drains these consumer products of their value within only a few years. This is especially true for commercial equipment such as kitchen or other devices. Consumer products aren't built for heavy use. They are built for once or twice per day, sometimes per week, usage. Commercial equipment, on the other hand, especially when it comes to laundry or kitchen commercial grade, are built for heavy, continual usage in a wide variety of formats.

That's why commercial equipment costs so much. The coils in a commercial laundry washer are worth more than that of its consumer grade counterpart. And it costs more to repair. And the cost per machine, especially when a consumer looks at a comparison between a consumer grade to a commercial grade, is about ten-to-twenty times in difference. This is why it is important to source actual commercial grade equipment for a business. And to do it on a cheaper manner than simply buying the newest machine.

The first piece of advice for any commercial grade machine purchase is to discover the power of auctions of commercial equipment or any used commercial equipment sales. You can do this via Facebook marketplace or online auctions. You will discover that you can get commercial grade equipment for laundry or kitchen at a much deeper discover, though some of the issues may require a bit of repair. Even hiring someone to fix a broken cold coil in a commercial grade used sandwich making station will yield out compared to purchasing a new commercial grade piece of equipment. New commercial grade equipment doesn't have that great of a shelf-life without maintenance anyway, and it is smart to use equipment that has been to hell and back, because you know that it can survive the rigors of real kitchen usage.

The thing that I mentioned previously with commercial grade equipment. No one really knows its value. You can usually talk down someone who has a pizza oven or proofing box, because they don't have a ton of buyers. They usually have one or two buyers at a time, therefore they are willing to off-load the equipment as quickly as possible, especially for cash. Typically, those who are listing the equipment are doing it as a side hustle, and are not the people who actually purchased it, but merely a third party willing to sell it. This creates the avenue of deal-making, especially if there is more business to be made.

Commercial grade equipment for the kitchen or laundry also comes with a price. You will need to use it in order for the investment to take off. And if you are attempting to start a kitchen, your county health department won't authorize consumer grade equipment for usage. So you're stuck with commercial grade, which are viewed as less likely to cause issues such as fires or breakdowns that can harm customers if they over-heat or they do not keep proper cold temperatures. Commercial grade equipment especially for food items, when keeping consistent temperatures, is viewed as more consistent than their consumer counterparts.

When you are looking over specific used items, you need to look for anything that can be viewed as a problem. Make sure to have it plugged in while you are there. If it is a cooling device such as a kegerator or refrigerator, ask that they do it twenty-four hours prior to your arrival. Also, look over any potential air leaks, or anything that will cause the system to cost you more in electricity than it's worth. All of these things matter because once you make the agreement, pay the person and part ways, you're stuck with whatever you've purchased.

A way around commercial grade equipment purchasing is to lease it. I recommend doing this for dishwashing machines or other heavy usage devices that you know will break down. For a monthly fee, the leasing company not only installs the commercial equipment, they service maintenance it as well supply the chemicals. There are some things that are well-worth paying a monthly fee for, especially when the alternative is a massive cost repair right when you don't have that amount of money. Larger office equipment fits into this category too; standup copiers and other devices that require several hours per visit for a service technician are more apt to be cost-effective when leasing rather than purchasing. The alternative is one breakdown and the bought machine is worthless until you spend several hundred more for someone to visit and fix repair it for you, without any guarantees of success. Plus, leasing companies often provide bulk supplies for their equipment, which they earn at steeper discounts than you can achieve on your own.

Commercial equipment auctions are their own segment of the industry. When you do bid on something, you are expected to go pick it up. Sounds easy enough except if it's a sink or something of value, that may be affixed still to the wall. This is where you need a good set of tools, work gloves and zero expectations that anyone at the commercial equipment auction will help you. Mainly because the auction pickup is often on site at a failed restaurant or place of business, and the people who are signing in/out are not there to help anyone. The money has already been collected, and they work mainly as a glorified administrative assistant coordinating winning bidders getting their stuff.

These types of auctions also gain certain benefits. As mentioned, people don't know what commercial grade equipment is usually worth. And several times, the winning bidders are looking for one item of interest, not several. That's why commercial sinks go for much less than they typically are worth. You can find a commercial sink for about 10 percent to 20 percent less than even on the used listed market, and a 3-pit sink, which is required of any restaurant by every health department in the United States, can go for about 30 percent to 40 percent of their used counterparts and well below the commercial grade new value listed by most companies. A lot of the industry is based on flipping too, much like shark residential real estate, where people don't know the actual value that you paid for the item, but assess on their own the value that they are willing to pay you as the middle man to buy the item from you.

When you arrive at these commercial auctions, you are often going to encounter several things. More bidders moving stuff out as quickly as possible, and late pick-ups or no-shows. That means equipment that was bid on, paid for, that the bidder just decided to not pick-up because they decided the ride to get it wasn't worth the price.

Some of this is caused by blanket bidding: the methodology of hitting the highest bid on every item of interest, only to discover that some of the bid items won are not worth the item and effort to pick them up. It's good to communicate with the commercial auction coordinator on site about any no-shows or late pick-up bidders, who have declined to grab the product but already paid for it. These items usually are given for free, as they become more of a problem to the auction coordinator than of value to anyone else but you.

These types of items can also be flipped in your area on craigslist and Facebook marketplace, simply with a description, a few photos from your smart phone, and a paid listing. Think of it as a quick flip: go for the easiest deal possible, and don't even try to deliver.

On these types of items, go a bit high on the ask, then you can be "talked down" by the buyer, in which you both get what you want. If you put the ask at exactly what the item is worth, you will end up being talked down below what you really want for the item every time. Everyone loves a deal. And they love to haggle.

SMALL BUSINESS SCHOOL

IMPACT FEES A.K.A. THE QUEST FOR MORE MONEY

City permits and impact fees are something to behold. There is always something which stops something else from occurring. There can be submission hearings based on the change of land-use, such as an office being converted into a restaurant if it's on the corner of a sidewalk. All of these come with permit fees, changing one designation to the other, which means the quest for more money. All of these city functionaries have to find ways to pay for themselves, and in doing so, charge fees accordingly. This is a continuous process. Along with impact fees, which suggests that if you pay $2,000 more in an impact fee, this will pay for whatever foot traffic impact you have on that area. It is, essentially, erroneous and more of a mechanism to stop/hinder progress rather than build it up.

The city permit and fee process slows down only so much of the entrepreneurialism of an area. If it is thriving, those who have the time, patience and willingness to pay for such permits get their way. Several ways to beat city permits is not to actually build anything. Instead, affixing things to walls or painting, instead of creating anything of a structure such as a wall or door, which allows a city planner to come through. City building inspectors will still demand to come through, and be unreasonable when you don't let them inside. You legally do not have to let a city building inspector inside, and can instead demand an appointment. They won't be happy about the law, but they will abide by it. Many times, they are on the quest for more money, especially during surprise inspections, in order to flag something that they demand you get a permit for, thus justifying their own existence by making you pay more into the city coffers. This is a big hinderance to small business owners, who do not fully grasp that there are mechanisms and jobs within the municipality who are there to flag any little thing possible, in order to extract $200 - $300 more in permit fees through the process.

There are several reasons why we do want credible inspections: Environmental health is one of them. We do not want people serving toxic food to the public because of food handling issues. Or alcohol poisoning because we did not have an investigative agency such as Liquor Control able to inspect their processes or report on serving minors or over-serving customers. However, this is not what often occurs in the world of weaponized permitting processes. Most of the permit fees are passed on costs by government entities who want to pay for budget shortfalls, but do not want to appear to raise taxes on the general public. So they raise fees such as permit or the notorious impact fees, and let the business community pass on the cost to their customers.

One of the most outrageous fee structures available is the impact fee. You will see this vary depending on the municipality that you reside in. Though there are some square footage measurements involved, impact fees can be completely illogical, and due up-front of the business even opening. A local laundromat owner was given a $100,000 up-front impact fee from his new laundromat site, even before turning on the water. This is part of the weaponization of the permit process. And a municipality can arbitrarily waive certain fees for certain businesses, such as the business & occupation tax (B&O), whenever it fees like.

B&O taxes are purposely mislabeled by elected officials. It is a ruse played on the public because B&O taxes do not have to be listed by businesses as a "pass off" cost in the same manner as sales tax. They are another tax on customers, yet customers have the misguided belief that businesses pay this tax. B&O taxes measure gross sales, not net sales. And as with anything, factor into the price of any item that the business is selling to the public. B&O tax revenues are often listed by the municipality in their budget in the same manner as sales taxes, with the direction of certain percentages going to specific items, such as fire districts. Yet, the public votes for B&O without as much inspection as they do sales taxes, which they know affects them. It is a shell game by governing bodies.

Grey water is something that needs to be treated. Municipalities typically want the businesses which create the grey water mess to be the ones which pay for the treatment of that water, so it can be recycled back into the water system. This is why waste water fees exist. And they can be exorbitant in certain situations. It is best to prepare yourself with a waste water fee schedule, so that you know the costs going into any project. Waste water fees are usually upfront as well. Meaning before you even use the system, you have to pay a large amount on the expectation of your usage. Then, if you go beyond that usage, you will be expected to pay another amount to shore up that deficit. This occurs whether you are a restaurant, a barber shop or a laundry.

The county will also provide you with an estimate at the time that you apply for a business license and health permit for the business location. When it comes to these calculations, they need to be provided into your sunken cost estimates. Because you will pay them. I knew a couple who attempted to get around the waste water fees in their community when attempting to build-out a coffee shop. What occurred is that they tended to avoid locations, then go upset when the county followed them around, ensuring that no matter what area they went, once they got their health permit, they would have to pay for the waste water fees. This happens a lot. People always think they can get around a taxation or fee, only to cost themselves more in the long run.

It is better to work with the area board that is making the decisions on waste water fee issues rather than simply attempt to go around them. Part of this is common sense that once you anger a municipality, the bureaucracy takes over and gets heated because you attempted to defy it. Instead, entrepreneurs when faced with these fees should be asking questions on how to make payment plans or other methods that weaken the overall blow of the entire fee cost. Waste water fees aren't going away. Especially if you are creating a large portion of the grey water waste. It is nonsensical to attempt to evade or avoid those fees when you are going to have to pay them regardless. Permitting fees don't change with the weather either. They are set there by county board and community representatives. When you see the waste water fees loaded up, you have to also assume that this is a by-product of shoring up budget holes elsewhere by the Public Utilities District (P.U.D.) and other government agencies.

Conversely, gaining a resellers permit is simply an endorsement on your business license. But it does carry a lot of weight when you purchase something that you intend to sell otherwise. Plus, it eliminates the upfront sales tax liabilities because you won't be keeping it long before you offload it. Resellers permits can also help you engage in online auctions, where you purchase equipment that you may have for a business down the road. You get to keep it, unused, during that period of time until you are ready to install it in any business you run, and only then are you liable for the tax owed.

A lot of this will be under-the-radar stuff anyway, specifically because it will be low items that the IRS won't really be looking it. With items such as vehicles, houses or boats, things which hold large tangible value, you have to be extremely careful of what you do with those items until you offload them for a profit. If you create a personal or business use for those items, no longer are they held under the resale rules, and you will owe taxes on their usage immediately. Everything is about finding new ways to charge you for something in case you manage to turn around and sell it. If you can't sell it, well, that's on you.

You will also need a resellers permit for anything such as alcohol or food sales, specifically because you won't be hit with sales tax on either item. Sales tax is essentially a collection by the end seller to the end buyer, leaving out the middleman. The end buyer which is the customer ends up paying the sales tax, with the exception of some items such as staple food, and it is collected by the business until it is turned over to the state. So, the business becomes the middleman in the entire endeavor.

A LESSON IN TAXATION, LICENSING AND PERMITTING

Prior to 2012, I was a babe in the woods when it came to understanding how municipalities and states weaponized permitting processes for small businesses. As with anything else, until you experience it, you think people who are going through it are being drama queens. Or they simply do not want to pay "their fair share." This occurs because everyone loves a discount only they get and a tax that they don't have to pay. There's a figurative milky cataract over everyone's eyes when it comes to these things, but when it comes off, it changes things, forever.

In September 2012, I was hired as the Director of Ticket Operations for the University of California-Davis. I put it as an update on my LinkedIn and received an inquiry from a business association meeting in Sacramento. They wanted to pay me $400 to speak at their conference. I thought that was a great idea, did the gig, filled out the W2 form at the conference and collected a check for $371 which included a 7.25% sales tax. I cashed the check into my personal account, forgot about it, and then received a letter in the mail from the state of California. Because I filled out the W2, I was required according to California law to form an LLC. I went through the process, and it cost me $426. Which meant it cost me $55 to speak at the conference. A few weeks later, I received a letter from the state of California's Franchise Tax Board. I now owed $800 annually as an LLC established in the state of California. Payable within 30 business days, otherwise I would be fined 5% per week along with other civil penalties. I paid the $800. Which meant I was now out $855 for speaking at the Sacramento conference.

I mentioned this to a colleague at UC-Davis. He referred me to a little old man in Sacramento named Colin who had previously worked for the IRS. He told me that I technically wasn't supposed to pay the $800 Franchise Tax fee the first year, but the state never tells anyone that just in case they'll pay it. Colin did my taxes, itemizing them, and it cost me $326. But I received a large amount back in over-payment to the IRS. To the tune of over $8,000. Years went by, but I continued to use Colin for my taxes. Then, in 2019, I was sent a letter by the IRS, proclaiming that my 2012 returns were being audited. The IRS decided that I owed that $8,000 after all. Colin told me that he would charge me $1,500 to defend the audit. I followed his lead. The IRS ended up sending me a letter stating that I owed nothing, that my audit was finished, and Colin was able to recoup his fees for me in my 2019 return the following year.

While this is a small example it is a glaring one of the hurdles that small businesses go through daily with taxation at the municipal, state and federal level. When the Biden Administration announced that they were adding 85,000 IRS agents, going after people not paying their taxes on generating more than $600 annually, it was small entrepreneurs with Etsy accounts that were targeted. Despite the nonsense from the Biden Administration suggesting otherwise, it is the smallest group, most likely not to be able to defend themselves legally with skilled accountants, who are hurt the most. It also woke me up as an entrepreneur. Anyone in the tournament should be awoken as well. Be prepared for the mental gymnastics that a government entity will go through in order to tax you more. Especially if you dare turn a dollar as an entrepreneur.

THE 24, 25x2, 26 MODEL

There is a total of 100% when calculating out your gross revenue. Now comes the interesting part to see if you've made any money (i.e. net profit). The 24, 25x2, 26 model of business has never failed me, or anyone that's used it. Never lose your shirt by the abhorrent belief that your percentages aren't an exact science. Should you choose to reduce one percentage in favor of another, the entire system that you have collapses entirely. Everything in this metric is about relationships to the other numbers involved. This metric allows you to protect yourself against wage waste (i.e. paying for unproductive staff hours) and/or price gouging your customers to the point where they do not return for repeat business.

The 24, 25x2, 26 model is simple: 24% of your gross revenue is dedicated to your labor costs (including payroll taxation). 25% is dedicated to restocking your shelves with product that you've sold. 25% is to cover all other overhead costs, including your lease, Triple Net, marketing, and other taxation such as B&O. Your final 26% is your net revenue, to re-invest in the business, or to serve as a cushion in case of emergencies. If you've noticed, I've used all 100% of the gross revenue up without mentioning actual profit. It is a vast luxury to ensure that you will make an actual profit, as things vary, but of that 26% net revenue, there should be some scraps for you to exist upon.

We've gotten away from understanding margins and how to cover a small business properly using gross revenue. The tech industry is somewhat to blame. That industry has used a "cash burn" model based off of spending through other investors money in order to produce a customer acquisition metric (i.e. what does it cost to acquire and re-acquire a customer to actual spend money). Cash burn rate exists because it is easy to spend someone else's money unaccountable to your own pocket book. Money gets wasted that way.

The 24% labor ratio is a hard standard. You should be able to detail out with your advanced scheduling all of the employees needed to produce the projected gross revenue for that week or month. There are always some variables, which is part of life. But if you are witnessing a 40% labor ratio, that should be a cause for concern. Labor ratios exist because the business has to make money, otherwise the jobs would also not exist. It is the inconvenient truth that general workers and those not in business do not wish to recognize. Sometimes, the taxation portion of 25% is a great indicator that you are in an area that does not respect nor understand business. Thus it might be good to know that in advance, calculate out the projected taxation, and see whether it is feasible to do business there at all.

YOUR BUSINESS PLAN

If you recall all of the nights of going through your business plan, then I have news for you. The moment you hit the street, it is likely irrelevant. Because market conditions often change as do consumer tastes. That is why you need to constantly update and redraft your business plan weekly until you are done with the business itself. Nothing stays the same forever, nor should your planning and projections. Everything should be fluid enough for you to properly understand and reaction accordingly.

And this is where the conversation gets really tough: Do you have a support system around you? This means a supportive spouse, children, friends, etc. Just because you are married doesn't mean that your spouse will fully support this endeavor. They may be wholly resistant, yet quiet when you start talking about going into business for yourself. Do you have people who are pushing you to become better, improve your economic outlook by working for yourself, or are they publicly or privately deriding your efforts? All of this needs to be placed in your business plan. It may seem odd, because no one wants to talk about it, but the bad actors who cause small businesses to fail are often internal. Frenemies that you are married to.

Your family needs to fully understand the business effort you are about to embark on. They likely will not. If you are seeking validation through conversation at Thanksgiving when you decide to start your small business, it may not be there. The art of dismissive people begins because most people are competitive for attention, especially in your own family. They may see your success as a threat to attention they get from other family members, exposing their accomplishments as less than yours. You have to be prepared for that. Some people tell you who they are, but present opposite actions. And what happens, through the measurement of time, is that the bad relationships will either drag you down or cause you to separate from them. No one likes this type of advice, but cutting out the negative sometimes means that you tighten your circle. And some people, even if they share your DNA, won't make it inside your circle due to their dismissive attitude on what you are embarking on.

Does your business plan have contingency in case you are unavailable to be a part of it? Do you have family members or loved ones who are willing to understand your business, to keep it afloat, if you have a medical issue? Are they willing or going to pick up the slack to ensure that the business itself does not fail? Sometimes, your living room or your spare bedroom or your garage is your home base of operation.

Will your spouse or loved one respect that decision? You may have to address the hostile actor living with you, who wants to throw out anything and everything of value. Baseball cards. Signed footballs. Even if it hosts or retains a specific value long-term, the hostile actor will not view it that way. Sometimes, it has less to do with the items and more to do with the idea that you bought it in the first place. Even if you packed all of it in a storage facility, suddenly, the hostile actor wants the storage facility off of the books. Some of this is a psychosis of control that has nothing to do with the business you wish to operate, but the lack of clearance from them to initiate the business in the first place. Your business plan should address these types of outliers.

Everything in your business plan should be about contingencies and getting you to think. There are lessons in everything, including that which you do not want to acknowledge or address. Those are the blind spots that wait to hit you, the second that you open your business. Your ability to recognize these holes and confront them head-on, should be aggressive and blunt. But they are also how you will broaden your scope in surviving as a business operator. Embrace the struggle. It forges you into a stronger person and business owner. Iron sharpens iron. People who take shortcuts are always going the longest road.

The Donner Party in 1846 decided to take a shortcut to get to California. They took off from Independence, Missouri through the Hastings Cutoff, which turned out to add four to six months to their journey. They ran through the baking hot Bad Lands and Rocky Mountains of Utah. Then they hit Nevada, right as winter set in. They ended up forging for food, finding none in the snow. And then they began their legend, as cannibals. All because they had to shortcut a wagon train instead of taking the full journey. This is a great lesson embedded in a dark story. Know how to avoid shortcuts that may end up killing your business in the end. Avoidance of risk is avoidance of knowledge, as we learn more from failures than we do from successes. I didn't just sit down and write this book, I had several books, different chapters, that came together to build this book. Because intention is often replaced by application, which humbles you on what you think you have, compared to what you end up having.

The real issue that you have to ask yourself to end this book is simple: Who is in your wolf pack? Who is ready to guide you forward toward small business success? At the end of the day, everything becomes tribal. Certain people will lead you to shortcuts. Others will hold you accountable. Focus on those who humble you, but in a positive way. Everyone is built to be an entrepreneur. The issue is whether they listen more to the "yes, but..." guy on their shoulder or the risk-taker on their other shoulder. Both can offer good counsel at times, or unnecessary advice that leads to heartache and ruin. Find your wolf pack, your tribe of people, and make sure that they lead to positive outcomes in your life. Chances are, you already know their worth. You just need to start listening, avoiding the shortcuts to small business entrepreneurship and success.

If that's not a solid business plan, I don't know what is.

OLD GROWTH

"In the end, it's not the years in your life that count. It's the life in your years." —
Abraham Lincoln

OLD GROWTH

It took me quite a while to process what occurred one night at Seattle University in the fall of 2006. Against Western Oregon University, SU played a Division II volleyball match of seemingly zero importance. Neither team had a winning record and was playing out the string. And then, Western Oregon's head coach, Joe Houck, took over the entire match himself, despite not being on the court or touching the ball. He created great theater. Stamping his feet, hitting the scorer's table, whatever it took to get the volleyball referee's attention.

This went on throughout the three games, which Western Oregon managed to sweep, simply because Houck's antics distracted the SU volleyball players and staff, who chose to watch him, rather than focus on the court action. Sometimes, you have to understand the game within the game. It was a risk that Houck was willing to take to get what he wanted: A win in an otherwise useless season. Houck went onto coach at the University of Portland for years prior to retiring. I doubt if he remembered the night against SU, but I did.

We create great theater in thinking we need sell entire product, rather than only parts of it. What if you only need to sell brake pads for a vehicle, instead of the entire vehicle itself? How does that change out your business model? Do you have the ability to source and distribute smaller, harder to find, items? That's a business. It is the firm understanding of reach dynamics, where small sources of income, or components of product, may actually be a better business model than the entire product put together. Think of Home Depot. It is 3,000 different companies distributing through a giant big box retailer. Home Depot is a conduit distributor for companies that merely make screws, or hammers, or nails. Yet, the greater theater image of Home Depot almost suggests that it makes all of those things, when clearly it makes nothing. It simply pays the lease, which holds the stuff made by others, and pays the employees to keep people from walking off with the stuff.

BUSINESS FINANCE FOR SMALL BUSINESS

You can knock out a lot of things, for several LLCs, within the same day or week or month, if you plan ahead. Every Sunday, I write down about 50-60 total goals for the upcoming week. This includes any meetings or mundane tasks that I will have. Then, I compile them into the first 2-3 days, knock out what I can on Monday-Wednesday, then parcel what is left on Thursday and Friday. Sometimes, I add more tasks during the week. But I usually knock out most of them, which can be for a variety of LLCs. If I have a small task with a candy company – checking on my candy route to refill machines at the local laundromat, I add that. The same with my publishing company, where I might write another chapter of this book or another book or work on the Amazon keywords to enhance its visibility within the Kindle ecosystem. The point is, little bits of time add up, and if you aren't screwing around, you can get a lot of things done quickly.

A lot of people will fixate on trying to get an SBA 3A Loan from a bank. They will work on brochures, business plans that are 50-60 pages thick and then they will get turned down by the bank. Unless they are willing to make that one LLC their full-time job as well as put up their house against the loan equity. Banks are essentially no-risk situations when it comes to start-ups. They don't like anything that hasn't been proven, or doesn't have something valuable aside from the start-up to leverage against. And they like to then criticize your business plan, as if they are somehow the line of demarcation between entrepreneurism and working for someone else. It is a fraudulent system, built off of the idea that you require massive amounts of money in order to start, and their clearance as a financial institution in order to get going.

This is really about a mindset. Even in the movie "The Founder" featuring Michael Keaton, the banks are turning down McDonald's because they don't care about the "Speedy Service System" that gets customers their burgers in 30 seconds not 30 minutes. They don't care about the volume of business that several of the McDonald's locations have produced. They care about the land, and more specifically, appraising Ray Kroc's house in order to give him a loan. That should tell you something about banks, and how they really feel about small business. SBA loans are simply the government confining you to one type of industry idea, locking you into a loan, against collateral, which is just your house.

My question is this: If your house is really the only difference-maker, and you've been looking at purchasing one, why not instead just save that money that you would pay toward a mortgage and rent a cheap studio apartment? Why not live without mortgage interest and other interest payments, in order to build your wealth without getting the house involved? Everything that goes wrong with that house, once you own it, you are responsible for. If you have an HOA, you have to pay to be part of it and don't have a choice. Same with that big muscle car that guys purchase to impress their friends. Why not actually sacrifice, save up, and really work on developing your business the way that you want to?

I'm not against lines of credit. I am against those who merely want you to put up your house so that they have an absolutely safe bet. In today's e-commerce world, we have Paypal and other lines of credit that will provide you with $7,000 - $10,000 loans with six months, interest free, in order to pay them off. So, let's suggest you start something small, which only costs $1,000 through PayPal credit. That means you have 6 months of $166 installments in order to pay off the $1,000 expense. So, your true number is at least generating $498 – a 3 to 1 return – which will accumulate $2988 against your $1000 loan in 6 months. The reason that you want at least a 3 to 1 return is due to several things: taxation, licensing, maintenance, etc. But also in case there is a 1-2 month period where you don't make that $498 or even $166, you still have the ability to pay off the entire $1000 expense without accumulating interest in the process.

Personally, I prefer automatic bank payments to creditors for the exact amount. Do not withdraw a $20 bill to pay $16.72 with. Somehow, that $3.28 will evaporate and go missing, thus you are out more than you needed to pay for. You want to have that debited amount go for the exact dollar figure, in order to protect the rest of the money in your account. This also helps during IRS tax time, as you are able to account for every cent brought in through credit and debits with a timed balance sheet. The bank account will always show the amount of money coming in as revenue, and it's your job to show the COGs associated with that account as a source of write-off. That's why having separate bank accounts is necessary, it makes it cleaner especially if an IRS audit comes around.

The IRS loves to audit businesses. Usually, they give a stack of IRS claims to a new associate, tell them to go after the business owner, and send out a nasty letter claiming that you owe a ton of money that you do not. My first audit was for my 2016 returns, for $8,800 that supposedly I owed. I received a notification in December 2018. I fought it because I had a bank account paper trail and could show every expense tied to it. I won. The IRS is not your friend. It is a government source of intimidation where they want to prove that you owe more taxation to the government, not less. Fairness is not an opinion with them. If you attempt to be reasonable, they will not. That isn't in their mindset. So, it matters that you account for a paper trail and know how you are breaking down everything in order to avoid more taxation.

Even if your product doesn't require a commercial leased space, it may require a different venue, such as a vehicle, in order to accomplish. A delivery driver for Uber Eats or Uber/Lyft ride sharing, means that you have to pay monthly installments for a fuel efficient car to drive people around in. That's a $500 to $600 automatic payment, excluding fuel, taxation, insurance and maintenance, as well as idle labor hours waiting for fares. Yet, because car loans are easier to gain, people consider it a startup to sign on the dotted line, and don't think about the costs incurred and whether or not they will yield out a decent profit. These car payments are unreasonably high because the cars are rolling off of the lot, brand new, with the whole "fuel efficiency" marketing behind it. Whatever you are saving in fuel, you are giving over to the car company in exchange for fuel efficiency.

The problem lies in the notion of how much usage you will get out of the car each day, committing yourself to becoming a driver. That means that instead of having several sources of income, you are still stuck with one, and because of the higher car payments, along with higher insurance payments because you are a commercial driver, as well as maintenance costs because the wear and tear of your car will be more, including the higher likelihood of flat tires, oil changes, etc., your costs are going to exceed your ability to generate a higher profit. This is where the idea of ride-sharing should become the idea of vehicle-sharing.

Consider that you may have a friend or neighbor with a hybrid car that may not always be used. Perhaps they have a third car in the household for two drivers, and they like to drive it occasionally. Why not work out a deal to lease the car for $200 - $300 a month, with the idea that you will only use it for a specific window of time; such as 4 hours each day during the week. The neighbor is responsible for any maintenance, but they do get to essentially cover half of their car payments each month through your lease. If you were to generate $25 in fares over those 80 hours, you would make $2000. Excluding $500 for fuel and oil changes, along with $300 for lease payment back to your friend for usage of his car, you would generate $1200. You still won't get out of insurance costs, but that likely leaves you with $1,000 in profit compared to a much lower one if you leased the car yourself. Plus, you get to write-off your mileage at the end of the year on your LLC for every fare that you performed during that time.

You may be able to even use an Exxon fuel credit card which has a percentage off per usage, and perhaps you work out a deal with a local oil change store based on frequency, in order to lower your costs there as well. It depends on whether or not you consider the entire operation that you are committing to as an ecosystem, not just a one-off transaction. Few start-up entrepreneurs would have gone to the level of trying to negotiate a deal with the local oil change store, and that's the point, you should always think about how many more side deals you can get in order to lower cost, driving up revenue.

What if you also decided to have magnet decals on your car, promoting the oil change business around town in exchange for a greater, reduced rate off of each oil change that you do? What if you also installed a digital car camera and took crazy footage of the traffic in front of you, logging each car accident or near miss, and uploaded it to your own YouTube channel to monetize it when you gain enough subscribers and generate enough viewership. That may be worth money there as well. What if you only chose to drive Uber/Lyft when the volume of fare traffic was at its highest, thereby gaining the most fares without idle drive time being possible, and then did something else during the low traffic times when no one wants a ride except the town drunk who wants to puke in your car on the way home from the bars at 3 a.m.

Speaking of which, I still do not understand bartenders who choose to work during the midday shifts when there are two people in the bar. That's when a novice or server should get those hours. Instead, a bartender only considers themselves honed for one job, not several. Nights should be reserved for bartending only when the patron volume is absolutely high, the tips are moving, and you can be utilizing the best portions of your work time toward the highest revenue generation possible. The other remaining hours should be where you work other jobs, which generate only higher revenue during those periods of time as well.

Consider that working part-time as a bartender, Uber driver and fitness instructor, only utilizing the highest shift periods to perform your work, may yield you thousands more per month than if you did all of them exclusively solo. It is up to you. A lot of people cannot handle the startup mindset of fractionalizing their committed time toward different tasks and businesses in order to generate the maximum amount of money possible. Thus they are victims to slow downs of an industry, because they committed to it, totally, rather than finding that they have much more available time to commit to things beyond work. That work-life balance actually occurs when you are less than fully committed to one job, and instead have the ability to do several small jobs at once.

A key reason to have separate bank accounts for every business, even the smallest one, is to showcase what your P&L is. Not just for your own accounting purposes, but to present to someone else who might want to purchase that business. They will want to see your P&L, and neglect on your tax deductions and depreciations over the years which have made your taxation burden smaller than the P&L shows. That's up to the new prospective owners to decide how to legislate their own tax obligations. They aren't going to see everything, including the small stuff, like writing down your mileage every time you go to your location of work, which can account for a 75-percent reduction of your taxation burden overall annually. Although business owners itemize, they tend to do so based off of the aggregate, such as leased space, and rarely think of the mileage that they can deduct for any business that they are conducting.

So too is the equipment that a business purchases, which can be depreciated over a 1-to-5 year cycle. Commercial equipment is very expensive when purchased new and is rarely worth it. The majority of new commercial equipment has an inflated price tag with a crappy warranty. It is better to look at used commercial equipment that businesses closing their doors are off-loading. That means hunting Facebook marketplace for deals. Same with online auctions, where everything is reserved as low as $1. Most of the bidding is fairly low even after close, with commercial 3-pit sinks, which retail at $800-$1200 new, going for $200. When you purchase used equipment, you also have the ability to do a quick depreciation of it for that tax year, then flip it to another one of your LLCs or sell it to another person's business at a used-retail price, and then depreciate the value again. There are ways to lessen your tax burden overall in commercial, which the average person will not understand. Commercial equipment is taxed as property by the county, on an annual basis. Thus, even after you purchase it, you need to pay an annual tax to have the ability to use it. Which is why you depreciate it below the value of taxation as quick as possible.

This speaks to one of the other things multiple LLCs can do for each other; have shared equipment. Perhaps there is a truck or trailer that is mainly purchased by one LLC that can be of part-time or single-use service to another LLC in your umbrella. This allows you to not have to rent equipment as often from others, but still create an invoice credit from one LLC to another, gaining a cost of goods credit without actually spending additional dollars. For instance, when my candy vending machines need to be deployed from Kirby Vending LLC to a new location, I need to use the Front Runner Media, LLC truck to deploy them. This creates both a mileage deduction, and invoice with COGs for the time. One LLC helps the other foster a deduction.

It creates a business ecosystem, allowing you to take advantage of situations and reduce taxation. Remember, this isn't you cheating anything. It is you figuring out ways to eliminate additional taxation burdens that are hell-bent on double-taxing you for usage. As if the government deserves to do so. These deductions, listed over LLCs and itemization, are available to anyone who wants to take the risk to create them, as well as generate the amount of time in order to do them. And if they don't, that's up to them. Complaining that businesses use tax laws effectively, such as the carry-forward ability of reducing taxation that larger corporations access, is both silly and wrong.

You always have a choice on how you want to conduct business. And you have a choice in how you want to view taxation, licensing and information. You can be dismissive or consider it wrong to use tax laws to your advantage. You can do so, pay more money to the government and gain less of a return, while working harder than everyone else. Remember, these laws exist for a reason, mainly because double-taxation is an illegality. But there's always a way to be double-taxed or continually taxed, over and over again, for the same item. It is your choice whether you wish to play the fool and pay it, especially when you are generating commerce while others are sitting at home refusing to do so.

There is also an art to how to pay your bills when you are a business. The general consumer pays a bill either with a credit card, thus owing a 28% annual yield percent (AYP) in interest against whatever they borrowed. But in the world of invoicing, businesses do have the tangible ability to use credit without the interest rate. The issue is that the windows are much shorter. A small business can get away with a 30-to-90 day aging cycle of invoiced materials. Depends on the company, but that allows the small business to turn around and sell the wholesale product at a retail price to the general consumer, thus making money before paying the original invoice. Yes, there is an art to it, but there is also some flexibility if you understand what you are doing.

While in the hard cider retail business, I would often look at the hard to purchase items that my customers wanted. Usually, they would be found outside of the normal distribution territories available in my area. Some were located more than 90-to-120 miles away (sometimes more than 500 miles from Olympia), in other states, such as Oregon, Idaho or Montana. I would plan out a "dock sale" with distributors in those states, whereas I would pick up the items on a rotating invoice, driving to the location, then hauling the product back to my Olympia store.

When I did so, I selected all of the hard to find items in advance, generally about $2,000 worth of wholesale cans. While driving to the distributor, I would have a special "alert" e-mail sent to my top 300-400 customers where they could pre-order the item. My goal was that out of 300-400 prospective customers, I would have 5% pre-order or 25 total pre-orders. My profit margin was close to 82% on each case. Keep in mind that where the distributor was located, the hard cider product was nearly underwater, because the availability wasn't scarce. In Olympia, the availability of those same hard cider items scarce, therefore it raised the overall value of the item.

Generally, upon returning to Olympia, I would average beyond 25 pre-orders and pay off the entire COGs of the items that I picked up. Then, everything from that point, was pure profit, which kept new customers arriving because they "heard" that I had a more extensive selection. The larger the selection, the more likely customers will seek you out trying to find some elusive item. This also feeds into the Amazon "long-tail" concept which has kept customers going back to their website for almost three decades. Amazon's "long-tail" is about having every item potentially available to you. The hard-to-find items will not be of equal inventory to the popular selling ones, but the items will still be there. It causes customers to not only seek out impossible-to-find items on the Amazon website, but also do all of their buying in general from that website. Why go somewhere else to piecemeal purchases found in one place?

This comes back to a common saying attributed to several originators: "Good artists create. Great artists steal." Leonardo Da Vinci, Pablo Picasso and Bill Gates each have been quoted originating that comment. What it means is that those who tend to borrow ideas and concepts from others for their own purposes also tend to develop more. Their work grows on the backs of others. Amazon's "long-tail" concept works in conjunction with the Toyota LEAN management style, which seeks to reduce waste of too much inventory, but also increase the efficiency of ordering the product. Amazon doesn't have too much inventory of the impossible-to-find items, but they do have some inventory of everything or the availability to locate it if someone wants to order it.

My late grandfather Cliff was a former accountant for the state of Washington's Department of Revenue. His "thriftiness" extended to his own personal purchasing habits. He would go to three different grocery stores over the price of toilet paper. He would buy the cheapest butter. Going through The Great Depression as a child had that effect on a whole generation. When I asked him what happened during his war service in The Pacific, he said, "we won," and left it at that. A crewman on the U.S.S. Andrew Doria, his ship was part of the Invasion of Lingayan Gulf from January 6 to 9, 1945. This was the landing that brought General Douglas MacArthur back to The Philippines. I tried to quiz my grandfather about MacArthur, but all he would reply was that "the man scared the hell out of me."

Cliff was a very good man, taught me a lot, especially about knowing how to treat others. In the late 1950s, he was sent to audit a black man's gas station in eastern Washington. He arrived, asked to see the station's "books" and was informed by the owner that, "Books? I don't know how to read." Cliff ended up taking a week off on his own time, caught the owner up on accounting, and never said a word about it. He did the right thing without an outlet to brag to social media, the newspaper or anyone else. He simply did it. I only found out about this story from my grandmother, because my grandfather wasn't one to talk himself up. Despite all of his experiences, he didn't brag about them. He didn't have to. He lived them out, then retired early from the state of Washington in order to work for himself. There is something about being able to work for yourself that matters in this country, and to not be locked into a job where you have to do the wrong thing all of the time. Another person in his role would have destroyed the gas station owner for not doing his own books or knowing how to process them. This is where government gets it wrong. Are public entities merely there to punish or are they there to help ensure everyone has a fair shot? Sometimes, it is difficult to tell.

I have an extreme dispassion toward those who prey on others. Multi-level marketing or "encouragement" seminars are some of those groups that I avoid. I recommend others avoid their lure of promising to have you quit "a job you hate" while also giving them $5,000 in payment installments in order to achieve that goal. You will find these MLMs and "encouragement" coaches lurking at chamber events and other avenues. They are there to separate you from your money and without any track record of success.

Any organization or "coach" who is there to make you feel terrible about your life choices is not your friend. Nor are they going to help you. Entrepreneurism is about independent motivation. You have to buy into yourself. In order to find yourself in the right place, ask yourself how the MLM benefits if you fail. Often, the MLM doesn't want you to succeed. They want to keep you on the tracks so that they can continue to milk you for more money. It is always recommended that you tend to frequent networking events but avoid the MLMs and "encouragement" coaches. When they have no tangible product, they eye you as stupid enough to still buy into their schemes. It is not worth it. No good can come of it.

THE SINKING SHIP OF PARTNERSHIPS

There are always blind spots with people you meet. Especially those you consider friends. It is due to the fact that you have built a trust and rapport with them. They stop looking at criticisms of your personal defects, and you do the same with them. It is natural, because as friends, all you care about is that relationship. But when there is skin in the game, things change, people are viewed as different, and their mindset toward work ethic changes as well. This is where you have to ask what you want out of a business partner. Do you need specifically to have a friend who becomes a business partner, and are you willing to separate the friendship from the business operations? It is very difficult to do, specifically because once there is skill in the game, the mentality toward effort and output changes drastically for both parties.

Business partners typically have issues of separation of labor. The way that they view labor, compared to the ideas that they bring to the table. You have to be sure that they are willing to actually put in labor hours, sweat equity without payment for their labor, and devote hundreds of hours with zero immediate return on investment. Those hours have to come from somewhere. Often, it is the removal of family time, or the ability to work another job somewhere else that actually returns immediate payment, that becomes a conflict. And there has to be a continual expectation that each member of the partnership will pull their weight, and contribute in the same manner. This is typically not the case, and can create negative feelings toward your business partner, which is why being friends, then business partners, may not work out for either type of relationship in the long run.

What exactly do you need with a business partner? Is it money? Is it labor? Is it business insight into the industry that you are going into? You have to figure out what their contribution is to the project. Many times, the business partner is shoring up a lack of your own personal interest in something that you need to make the business run. Resources such as financial backing tend to come with their own costs, such as the business partner's inability not to accept free product whenever they or their family/other friends come into the place of business. Or it might be you that believes in this sort of faulty logic. Either way, a determination as to why you actually need to have a business partner needs to be penciled out.

In the end, consider that you are essentially financially married to this person. And sometimes marriages start with two lovebirds and end with two bloody bodies thinking the other one is evil. A lot of friendships turned business partners end up killing both, and then taking years to recover a relationship if at all, long after the business is no longer in existence. Avoiding this would mean examining the entire business relationship prior to developing your own business and whether or not you can sacrifice your friendship in the process. You have to know whether your partner, or you, are really interested in another full time job. You have to know whether your spouse, or their spouse, who are both business partners themselves, are willing to sacrifice time with you for the sake of the business. These are factors only considered long after the commercial lease is signed, and there is no way to divorce quickly if the entire project isn't going to work out. It is a mentality of what really business partners want when examining whether to actually try to generate money together.

You have to determine whether you are seeing a flash of interest or the reality of a business partnership. Can this person actually deliver on their end? Can you deliver on yours? Holding yourself accountable is part of this assessment. As is whether the business partner can do the same of themselves, and both of you to the other. It gets complicated because everyone has to factor in whether they have the cache to call each other out for misgivings or issues when it comes to business, and whether working together is really in the best interest of the friendship. Specifically because the friendship was the original bond, and was not financial at all. The question comes down to a larger one: Are you both on the same page on how to run a business in general? The answer from your business partner may surprise you.

Partnerships are about delivering on your promises to another person. Specifically, follow-thru, which doesn't happen as much as you would think. Partnerships where there are married couples with zero kids and a single person with three kids, can dissolve quickly. Mainly because the person with the kids has commitments already set in motion. They may not see those Friday and Saturday nights working at the business to be a commitment they can make, specifically because that's when they have their kids every other weekend. This should be resolved long before you actually start your business with anyone else. More specifically, what are the outside commitments that the other person will have that will impact the business you are thinking of starting with them? People with kids tend to want to spend time with them, or have no choice but to spend time with them, and that means a time commitment away from working the business, especially a storefront, when they might be needed the most.

When you have blind spots of your friends, they make bad business partners. They will do things that they expect you to look past, make decisions without you, and be a bit nefarious. Or you will do it to them. It comes down to the adjoining work ethics and whether they are actually aligned between you and them. What you trusted before was not in a business relationship. You never had to look at their warts. You never had to look at their flaws. Nor did they have to look at yours. When the curtain is drawn back, and you see who the other person in the business relationship is, you may not like what you see. Ethics are a big one. Also following through with promises and commitments is yet another.

You should consider taking a partnership inventory prior to actually becoming a partner with anyone. Is this a good person? Not just a good business person, but a good, ethical person that you can trust? Again, why do you need them? What resource are they delivering that you cannot provide or learn yourself? Conversely, why do they need you? When you are dealing with spouses and other outside parties, you may find that you are the one who will be forced out of the business partnership or viewed as less than equal at a certain point. Remember, everyone is a hero in their own story, therefore the villain has to be someone else. Even if the viewpoint is inaccurate.

Part of the blind spot of a friendship is not knowing someone else's financial situation or position. Are they over-leveraged with mortgages, credit cards and defaults on previous loans? Are they the type of person who is going to commit shady activities at your business, and risk the LLC itself of being in the crosshairs of federal, state or local officials? It depends on whatever side activities they are a part of. Those side activities you may have never known about, because you had a blind spot as a friend for them.

A larger factor is whether you want to be married to their personal brand. What they post on social media, who they are in the community, instantly reflects on you, both positive and negative, when you are their business partner. How do they treat employees or you in a work environment? What is their viewpoint on investment? I have a friend who is constantly eager to start businesses as long as they are minimal risk. He will get up to the edge, then talk himself out of it because he starts thinking of the idea of losing money in the process. You have to be ready for these types of factors when deciding to become someone's business partner.

Business partners sometimes have the notion that they are not going to put in sweat equity, or work the job. Instead, they are providing capital. They are an investor, where if they put $5 in the machine, they expect $20 to come back out at a 4:1 return. This is something that you should know in advance. Especially if you are selling them on the idea that as business partners, they won't be working the job or that it will be an easy job. Everything seems easy, until someone has to put on their socks, shoes and drive down to the storefront to work a Friday or Saturday night. Then it becomes a commitment and has a lot of its own feelings as a part of it.

You may feel that this is obvious. That they would want to protect their investment the same as you would. But that may not be so. People have differing viewpoints on things. When something isn't realized, they are less protective of it, and when it is realized, they may want to make decisions without you in the picture at all. Again, this comes down to the blind spots of not truly knowing the partner(s) that you are going into business with. Another factor is what if they quit on their investment entirely? Such as not showing up. Without notice, they disappear or decide not to continue on with the investment. What happens then? This happens frequently in small business, where partnerships are less apt to have willing partners. And yet, if you turn around the business by yourself, they are still investors/owners in the business and may come back, staking a claim that they deserve full share rights, despite abandoning the project earlier.

Verbal handshake deals are worthless. They do not require any follow-thru or legality to ensure that they are carried out. Verbal agreements are shitstorms waiting to occur. It is best to get an operating agreement in place. Something that ensures that there are benchmarks, expectations, divisions of labor and other guidelines in place. If a marriage doesn't work out, there are guidelines such as laws put in place for a divorce. A business operating agreement is no different. People need to ensure that they know specifically where they stand. Note in the previous paragraph, I mentioned abdication of a business by one partner. Bet your eyes rolled at the notion of that abdicating partner returning after the business has been built up to re-stake their claim. Unless you have an operating agreement with established abdication rules, there is nothing stopping the abdicating partner from returning for full equity at their choosing. That is why an operating agreement matters. It kills the verbal agreement shitstorm which has no legal backing in court.

Operating agreements are not sexy, but they have teeth. Especially when your business partner decides to perform on the four-hour work week principle. Meaning that they are involved themselves for less than four hours a week in matters concerning the business, and the rest of the time, not do anything at all. There is a difference between those who work for themselves and those who have only worked for others. Working for yourself prior to starting a business with someone else means that you've only eaten what you've killed. If you don't make a sale, you don't make money. Folks who have only worked for others have never really risked, but have always received a reward. It has made them slow and lazy when it comes to understanding what it takes to generate $4 from $1 of investment.

This comes to working with suppliers, not buddies as well. Your partner may only want to reward nearby friends as part of their efforts, but it may not actually yield out for the business at the lowest possible price for the same per unit cost. In fact, it may be the highest. Suppliers who are buddies tend to jack up the price, knowing that you will pay for it without question of searching around for a better price overall. Suppliers have a tendency not to service accounts effectively if they think that they've "got you" (i.e. they don't feel you have or will go anywhere else but them). You should ensure that suppliers know that they aren't the only game in town, and if they aren't providing great customer service, you will head elsewhere with your business. This is also true of the account reps for suppliers. Sometimes, you have to consider going over their heads, speaking to their supervisor, if they are not servicing the account effectively. If your supply delivery days have changed from weekly to bi-weekly to monthly, without your authorization or notification. Sometimes, ensuring that the supervisor of the supply company knows that you will spend more, if you have the ability to, can create more avenues to increased delivery days.

This is all about creating a brand. Usually, brand building is discussed when measuring out a B2C relationship. But it can be B2B as well. How suppliers treat you is how they view your brand. If a supplier has a tendency to ignore your business when it comes to special deals, or new items on the catalogue where you might have a first shot at purchasing them, this is an issue. It means that they do not view your brand as effective or worth their time. This can be an opportunity cost for you down the road, when your competitor is treated better by a supplier than you, and can offer not only more cost-effective products, but also higher quality or special run products that you have not been offered at all.

Part of that brand creation comes from you as a business person. What do you stand for? Are you a person of integrity? Do you know your numbers? Or are you just really hanging out on Daddy's money? One of the biggest issues is how you are viewed not just as a boss but as an entrepreneur. Are you someone that others would say is a great entrepreneur, or someone who is merely in charge because they were born into the family business? One method that family-run businesses do in order to prepare their next generation for leadership, is to have those children or off-spring work for someone else. That way, they cut their teeth in the same industry, but without the ability to move up unless they earned it. Later, when they are hired back by their family business, they are at a higher level, because they have earned it elsewhere. It helps with both their own personal self-worth as well as that of the support of the employees who may not be family members but make the business survive.

This type of brand building extends to those you are partners with in a business. Are they people who treat employees well? Do they know their numbers? Are they someone who lies, cheats, steals or merely acts like a hardass and ruins every relationship around them? Again, this might be a blind spot that you carry if you don't notice how they treat others. Their reputation once married with yours ends up becoming yours. It matters who they are, who they say and what they do, because it becomes who you are in this business, even if that partner is gone later on because it didn't work out. Be careful who you align with, as their brand merges with yours, for better or worse.

If you do have a physical business such as a warehouse or retail or restaurant or office, you should consider having security cameras. Sometimes, it's more for your partner and employees than the customer. Especially if you have a safe, or something that can be moved quick. While it seems horrible to consider, all it takes is a bad argument or a stressful day where the need is great, for someone to decide to steal. They can say that they will pay it back all they want, the fact is, once they cross that threshold of a breaking point, they are no longer the person that they were previous. They have lost their integrity by stealing. Regardless of the reason. And having a security camera locked onto the safe or areas of interest is important. Getting a security camera on a 30-day digital video loop is also a way to create threat versus reality scenario. If everyone thinks that they are being recorded, the chances of theft are less overall.

You should always take a partnership inventory, as mentioned previously. Avoid the idea of theft against the business by knowing who your partner is, as well as who they might hire. They might be swell people who would never steal a dime, but they might also over-buy or under-supply the business out of human stupidity or an aversion to spending money. That doesn't make them bad people, but you should know who they are, be on the same page with their mentality toward business, and generating money overall. Otherwise, it will not work out. You two will be fighting most of the time, and it will lose you more money than it gains.

Notice that I referred to over-buying or under-supplying the business as a factor. It happens more than theft. But it is just as costly. If you have a partner who has signature authority with a supplier and is over-buying product, or purchasing product that no one really wants, but that the partner personally likes, that can be an issue. The same with under-supplying for a business. When a customer walks into the business, yet cannot find what they are looking for because there is little to no inventory on a product that they want, you've lost not only that customer but several others. Word gets out quick on what you don't have, especially if it's something that customer demand is in the mood for.

That partnership inventory should also consider if they actually understand their competitors. How they feel about expansion, or anything else. And it needs to be solidified with a partnership operating agreement. If you don't have an operating agreement with a business partner, you will end up being screwed. That's why handshake or verbal deals don't work out. Because anything goes when people are legally at each other's throats, and what was promised verbally or handshake is essentially worthless.

If a business is worth doing, it's worth having a lawyer to write up an operating agreement when it comes to two or more partners. Laying everything out on the page, written by a lawyer in the state to which the business is born. That last part matters, because legal advise and contract writing by a lawyer needs to be performed in the state where they have passed the bar, otherwise it might not be recognized at all. Operation agreements should also spell out how to get rid of a partner or dissolve the partnership if matters don't work out at all. While these things aren't fun to think about, they are important when investing money together.

This may seem a tad extreme, but hiring a private investigator to understand who your partner is, should not be out of the realm of possibility. PIs can turn up many things, including bad credit histories, complaints by former business associates, and other matters that your potential future business partner isn't or won't tell you about. The truth is, people lie about a lot of things. They lie about things that they do, as well as things that their spouses or kids do. Even if those things affect you directly. It is much better, prior to actually getting into business with someone, to have the full, unadulterated picture of who the person is, regardless of whether they fail to mention something or not.

The PI game is something that should be taken seriously. You are bonding yourself to another person's financials by joining them as a business partner. This goes beyond branding your reputation with theirs. Does your partner actually have the liquid capacity that they say that they do? Sometimes, they don't, and they tend to shirk on mentioning this until you are far down the road of signing a personal guarantee for a commercial lease. Or they have bad credit or a DUI or something that could damage your standing with a state agency licensing body. You should know these things upfront, go in eyes-wide-open and understand that people will keep things from you, even if you are the best of friends and if they claim to want to be good business partners overall.

Having a legal operation agreement is not uncool. It is not unsexy. Nor is it bad for business. Especially if you are getting involved with a family member, or in a family business. People who share the same DNA often screw each other most. They do it because they feel that they can get away with it. Or they justify it as they are family, so you are stuck with them. If you get family involved together even in a family business, they will often not play fair when it comes to percentage cuts of the business for a variety of reasons. Not having a legal operation agreement, or contract of the division of labor/expected pay, etc. is a recipe for disaster.

And whether you want to recognize it or not, your business partner, even if they are not a DNA relative, will have a life that will involve you. Their spouse is your business partner. Their kids are now your business partner. A legal operation agreement also spells out what occurs if your business partner cheats on their spouse and gets a divorce. The same is said for you, and your love life. If you get a divorce, it affects your business partner as well. If either you or your business partner dies, the agreement spells out who gets what within the business. And this matters because it affects more than just you two. It affects your employees' livelihoods, suppliers, landlords, customers, etc. All of that should matter as you look to move forward on a business arrangement.

Spelling out the bigger issues means that you won't complicate the simple, but also won't simplify the complicated. Whether that is marriage struggles that emerge when co-working a business during a partnership, or being the best of friends, worst of business partners, everything can be easily written out when it comes to the division of labor and expectations of involvement in the business. This is necessary for people not only to understand how to earn their keep, but also from claiming that they are doing enough when clearly they are not. What happens when a business partner has kids, when it comes to time-managing their role within the business and their responsibilities as a parent? Often, the business gets the short-end of the stick, and one of the business partners, especially if there is a childless partner, feels that they are putting in more effort than the partner more willing to spend time with their children rather than helping the business grow. This is not to be heartless toward children at all. But it should be known, upfront, how the business will be treated when there are other demands on a business partner's time and effort.

A legal operation agreement helps both you and your business partner, or many partners, lay out the long-term commitment expectations that are had of everyone who signs that document. It not only creates expectations, but understands and defines expertise, along with sweat equity toward the business. The idea of sweat equity, beyond liquid capital, is what will make your business thrive. Anyone can spend money. But it takes a real master to input the sweat equity which will push the business further. If you choose to forgo a legal operation agreement for the benefit of saving a few bucks on a lawyer to draft one up, you will go forward at your own peril and spend far more if and when the business arrangement doesn't work out, wishing that you had spoken to a lawyer at the start of the business in the first place.

TAKING THE "L"

Sometimes, divorces occur when you least expect it. It is no different with a small business. When the business is failing, becoming too much of a sinkhole, entrepreneurs make too many attempts to stick it out. And dig themselves deeper into debt. Some business models will not work out, no matter how great the idea is. Dumping more money into something that customers reject, is anti-thetical to the idea of commerce. Yet, while things happen, including shit decisions which cause the business to fail, some folks will not admit it. There are divorced couples where one person still thinks the other person is always going to come back, despite that other person engaged or re-married. When it fails, take the "L" and say "it's time" and close the doors to that business. Always write down what went wrong, along with what went right, and learn from it.

There is no perfect model or situation to anything. Small business is a big gamble. But so is living an ordinary life, where you work at a job until they lay you off or you get retired. Sometimes you misread the market, or cannot achieve what people before you achieved. I sold The Cider Barrel in the summer of 2023 to a young mother who got a great price. I trained her, was on-call for about 3-4 months, and I thought she would make it. By 2025, it was closing. Divorce and other issues had occurred. The City of Olympia pushed a $24 per hour minimum wage, which scared off any buyers. The market changed on her overnight. I was able to work the business in several ways, that because of her family, she decided she could not.

When you purchase someone else's business, you are also buying into their promises and legacy. There are always black holes to the business. There are always issues unaddressed because it all will cost you money. You are buying "as is" when you sign the legal agreement to transfer the sale. The e-Gaming trailer that appeared at our semi-pro soccer games tried to get me to sign an NDA before he would let me see the books. Wanted to have me over for dinner to discuss. This type of behavior is about clouding the issue, much like a realtor does. Gets you excited so that you do not look in-depth into what you are buying. One of my friends owned a building that rented space to an ice cream shop, whose owner wanted to sell the business. The friend asked me to look over the P&L. Took me two minutes to see that the ice cream owner was withdrawing all of his liquid capital from the business. Another two minutes to see how all of the machines weren't being serviced or were ready to be replaced under the timeline of the ice cream shop's franchisee agreement with the franchisor. These are the little things that you should prep for ahead of time.

And if you sell a business, you will always be the bad guy if the new owner fails. I have had mixed results with new owners of businesses that I have sold them. Sometimes, they get it and take off. Other times, they collapse under the weight of their own ego or lack of industry depth. When you purchase a business, you better be almost willing to engage as if it's a college-level course. People refuse to do that or adapt their lifestyle. When they purchase a business, they are doing so under the auspices that they do not have to do the hard stuff in order to succeed. The issue is that the selling owner may have a following or insight that the buying owner refuses to learn or build upon. And that is when troubled waters emerge.

WE ARE ALL ON STRINGS

There is no safe job or safe industry. COVID-19 and the subsequent government shutdowns of 2020 taught us that. Every job can be ended because of arbitrary reasoning. Every business can be shuttered, or be made "essential," through some government mandate. The idea that your business model might fail, not because of your own doing, but because of outside forces, should be a consideration in any endeavor you partake in. Faced with that reality, it should help you pivot and sustain yourself, making your business stronger in the process. Even if that the new business model looks nothing like the original business model you started with.

A few years before 2020, I worked as a videographer for the

Washington State Legislature. I was told to host a livestream on Facebook and brought the streaming camera into the Senate Caucus room. The staff showed me which Internet plug to insert the streaming camera into. Within five minutes, a team of Capitol I.T. staff ran into the room. My streaming camera had shut down the Internet for the entire state legislature and Governor's Office. That was when I realized how easy it was to shut down a state government's Internet access, and that we were all on strings. Pull one string, the entire shirt turns to threads.

I mention this as a way of ending this book. That no matter how much information you pour into your business or your craft, there will always be some pessimism lurking around the corner, the potential of failure awaits. However, think of the possibilities of not doing your business idea. Think of how you will have otherwise felt then, knowing what could have been, if only you had decided to risk rather than play it safe. Especially when the next COVID-19 type government shutdown occurs, and you lose your "safe" job working for someone else anyway. We're all on strings at every job, whether we work for someone else or ourselves. We might as well roll the dice with some risk, and see where the dice lands. May the odds be ever in your favor when you take a chance on yourself.

Muzzle the "yes, but..." guy on your shoulder for a bit. He's talked enough. Ask yourself if the risk-taker on your other shoulder is right. Chances are, he has a valid point or two. Do everything in measure, but realize there is a cost to everything, including when you do nothing. After all, you invested in the book hoping to learn something. Because you were desperate to seek it out. Whatever that was, hopefully you've found it. Welcome to the path of starting a small business. The road is a lot longer than you expected, but that's a good thing. It means you are learning in the process.

www.ingramcontent.com/pod-product-compliance
Lightning Source LLC
Chambersburg PA
CBHW020154200326
41521CB00006B/368